FRESHWATER FISHES
of Eastern Canada

BY W. B. SCOTT

Curator, Department of Ichthyology and Herpetology
Royal Ontario Museum

Photographs by W. H. Carrick

formerly Executive Secretary
Ontario Waterfowl Research Foundation

FRESHWATER
FISHES

of Eastern Canada

Second Edition / University of Toronto Press
Toronto and Buffalo

ACKNOWLEDGMENTS

PUBLICATION of the first edition was facilitated by the interest of the Carling Conservation Club in the zoological research of the Royal Ontario Museum.

With few exceptions the photographs of the fishes shown on the following pages were taken specifically for this work by W. H. Carrick and most of the fishes were photographed when alive. The photograph of the shad was donated by Dr. V. D. Vladykov, Department of Fisheries, Quebec, that of the pink salmon was taken by Mr. Leigh Warren, Royal Ontario Museum, and that of the tiger muskellunge by Dr. G. S. Cameron. Dr. V. D. Vladykov, now of the University of Ottawa, Mr. Vianney Legendre, Ministère du Tourisme, de la Chasse et de la Pêche, Québec, and Dr. G. H. Lawler, Fisheries Research Board of Canada, generously provided information and specimens for photographing, and I am most pleased to acknowledge their help. Mr. T. H. Turner, Department of Fisheries, Ottawa, kindly permitted use of the photographs of both species of *Fundulus* and blackspot stickleback.

I am grateful also to Dr. P. F. Elson, Mr. R. A. McKenzie, Mr. J. W. Saunders, and Dr. M. W. Smith, members of the staff of the Biological Station, Fisheries Research Board of Canada, St. Andrews, New Brunswick, and Mr. V. R. Taylor, Department of Fisheries, St. John's, Newfoundland, for information on the fishes in their areas.

I am especially grateful to the many fishery biologists on the staff of the Ontario Department of Lands and Forests, especially J. W. Christie, R. G. Ferguson, N. V. Martin, R. A. Ryder, and the late John Budd.

I would like also to express my very sincere thanks to the many commercial fishermen, sports fishermen, fellow fishery biologists, naturalists, and students who have used the earlier edition of this book and have offered valuable suggestions and advice. In particular, I am happy to acknowledge the suggestions and advice of my colleague, Dr. E. J. Crossman.

And finally, I must acknowledge that neither the original edition nor this revision would have been completed without the skilled technical assistance of my wife, Milly.

W. B. S.

CONTENTS

INTRODUCTION   vii

INTRODUCTION TO SECOND EDITION   x

AUTHOR'S COMMENTS, 1972   xi

ILLUSTRATION OF EXTERNAL PARTS   xii

ARRAY OF FISHES with illustrations   1

Lampreys—Petromyzontidae   2
Sturgeons—Acipenseridae   7
Paddlefishes—Polyodontidae   8
Gars—Lepisosteidae   9
Bowfins—Amiidae   11
Herrings—Clupeidae   12
Salmons, trouts, chars, and whitefishes—
     Salmonidae   15
Smelts—Osmeridae   32
Mooneyes—Hiodontidae   34
Mudminnows—Umbridae   36
Pikes—Esocidae   37
Suckers—Catostomidae   42
Minnows—Cyprinidae   50
Catfishes—Ictaluridae   71
Freshwater eels—Anguillidae   76
Killifishes—Cyprinodontidae   78
Cods—Gadidae   79
Sticklebacks—Gasterosteidae   81
Trout-perches—Percopsidae   85
Basses—Serranidae   86
Sunfishes—Centrarchidae   89
Perches—Percidae   99
Silversides—Atherinidae   114
Drums—Sciaenidae   115
Sculpins—Cottidae   116
Flatfishes—Bothidae and Pleuronectidae   120

KEY TO: Families   121
         Salmons, trouts, chars and
             whitefishes—family Salmonidae   123
         Minnows—family Cyprinidae   124

FURTHER REFERENCES   128

INDEX   129

INTRODUCTION

THE TERM, eastern Canada, is here meant to include the provinces of Newfoundland, Prince Edward Island, Nova Scotia, New Brunswick, Quebec, and Ontario. The combined area of these six provinces is more than 1,000,000 square miles. In this region there occur, or have been reported to occur, 154 species or kinds of freshwater fishes. The greater number of species have been reported from Ontario (135), while Quebec (101) comes next and New Brunswick (46), Nova Scotia (34), Newfoundland, and Prince Edward Island follow in order. The last two provinces, having a predominantly marine environment, have only a limited freshwater fauna.

The purpose of this book is to provide game and commercial fishermen, as well as all others interested in fishes, with information concerning the freshwater fishes that occur in eastern Canada and, also, to assist in the accurate identification of the various species. Technical language has been avoided wherever possible but no loss in accuracy has resulted because of this. Altogether, 154 species have been given consideration, representing the fishes occurring in the fresh waters of the region. The general plan of treatment for each species was decided upon because it seemed to be the most concise and readable way to present the necessary information.

The arrangement of the various species of fishes is one which is well known to fishery biologists and zoologists generally but is probably not known to others. The system is simply one of placing the most primitive, i.e. less specialized, fishes first and the most highly developed fishes last. The lamprey, which lacks true jaws, paired fins, bony skeleton, and many other features of specialization, is placed before the whitefish. The whitefish, lacking spines in its fins and possessing an open duct from the throat to the air bladder, is considered to be less specialized than the largemouth bass. Considerations such as these have determined the arrangement of the fishes on the following pages. Artificial keys to families, and the more difficult species appear on pages 121–27.

EXPLANATION OF THE HEADINGS AND TERMS

Names: common and scientific

Heading the write-up of each species on the following pages is the common name recommended for use by the American Fisheries Society, published in 1960 under the title of *A List of Common and Scientific Names of Fishes of the United States and Canada.* It is hoped that the present work will assist in the wider acceptance of these names. For some of the lesser known species the Society has not recommended common names, in which cases the most widely used names for those species have been selected. Under "Other common names" are listed names by which the particular fish is known in different parts of the country. This is not intended to be a complete list of all the local names by which the fish is known. The French common name is entered last.

With a few exceptions, the scientific names used are in accordance with the nomenclature employed in the 1958 edition of the *Fishes of the Great Lakes Region*, by Drs. C. L. Hubbs and K. F. Lagler. The scientific name is included because it is the only name by which the particular species can be accurately designated. The name consists of two parts, both latinized, the first part known as the genus or generic name and the second part, properly known as the trivial name, sometimes called the specific name. Use of the same generic name for two fishes indicates close relationship; thus many different species of minnows have the same generic name, e.g. *Notropis*, and they are closely related. The generic name can be compared, then, to a family name (e.g. Smith), the trivial or specific name to a Christian name (e.g. John). The name of the man who first described the species follows immediately after the scientific name. It is called the authority. If the generic name used by the original describer has been changed, the authority is given in parentheses; if not, the name appears without parentheses.

Distinguishing features

This section, when combined with the illustration, contains sufficient detail to permit accurate identification of most of the fishes treated in the present book. Certain species, particularly some of the minnows as well as many of the fishes which are not illustrated, are difficult to identify, but a key to the minnows is provided for the serious student on page 124. Fortunately, many of such species are of rare or of restricted occurrence and, therefore, they will not likely be encountered by most fishermen.

Size

Unlike the warm-blooded birds and mammals, which reach an adult size and virtually cease to grow, fish continue to grow throughout their lives. Granted the rate of growth diminishes rapidly after the first few years for most species, but growth does continue. In addition, since some waters are more productive of food or possess other advantages, fish in some lakes grow at a more rapid rate and reach a larger size than fish from other lakes. A smaller size may also result from overcrowding. Whatever the reasons, fish do vary greatly in size, especially over such a large area as eastern Canada, and the average size given is intended only as a guide. The maximum sizes, however, are as accurate as possible with the information at hand. Wherever more accurate information is possessed by the reader, it is urged that he communicate with the author or write directly to the Royal Ontario Museum.

Occurrence

The statements of occurrence for the various fishes are based on information gathered from the collections of fishes and scientific records of museum collections and field experiences of the author. This is believed to be the most accurate and up-to-date information available. For most fishes only the occurrence in eastern Canada is given but, with only a few exceptions, the fishes listed occur in other parts of North America. Most of the species occur in the United States and many also in central and western Canada. In general, those species that have been noted to be *rare* in eastern Canada are actually southern forms which reach their northern limit of range in southern Canada, particularly in the Lake Ontario, Lake Erie, and Lake Huron drainages of Ontario.

Life history and habits

In most cases only a limited amount of information has been given in this section, in part owing to limits of space but owing also, in many instances, to a lack of information. The life history for many species of eastern Canadian fishes is far from complete. Except where otherwise stated, spawning dates given apply to southern Ontario. The region under consideration is so large that there will of necessity be considerable differences in the spawning dates between southern and northern localities. For example, the yellow perch may spawn in Lake Erie in May, a full month before the same species will spawn in the Hudson Bay region of Ontario.

Food

Unless otherwise stated, only the food of adults is considered under this section. The food of most animals varies greatly with size, age, or season and this is also true of many fishes. Thus, almost all young fishes eat minute plants and animals (collectively referred to as plankton) but as they grow larger their food habits may change considerably. For example, in the case of the northern pike and the shallowwater cisco, both as young fish may eat very similar foods but as adults they differ greatly since adult pike live almost entirely on fishes and other vertebrate creatures, while the cisco continues to feed principally on plankton.

The feeding habits for most of our fishes are not at all well known, although for some of the important game and commercial species a great deal of information is accumulating. However, the food relationships of the various fishes found together in one body of water will undoubtedly present a complex picture that will require a great deal of research work before a clear understanding is obtained.

Comments

Under this title have been grouped remarks dealing with such characteristics as flavour and appearance of flesh, and importance as a game, commercial, or bait species or as a forage fish. The term "forage" in this case refers to the value of the particular fish as food for other fish.

From the foregoing remarks it is obvious that a great deal remains to be known about fishes. There are many more fishermen than there are fishery biologists and these fishermen invade almost all known bodies of water in the region. They constitute an army of observers whose observations could be of great assistance. Anyone who has information concerning the occurrence of fishes which are said on the following pages to be rare, or knows of the occurrence of fishes in parts of the region other than those stated, or has caught an unfamiliar fish and wishes to have it identified, should communicate with the Royal Ontario Museum. Preserved specimens of fishes are much more satisfactory for identification than verbal descriptions. Fishes are easily preserved by immersing them in a 10 per cent solution of formalin (obtainable at most drug stores) which can be prepared by mixing one part of formalin with 9 parts of water. Fishes over 8 inches or so in length should have a slit made in the right side to allow the solution to enter the body cavity and so preserve the internal organs more quickly. If formalin is not available fish may be heavily salted to prevent decomposition until more careful treatment can be given. Alcohol can also be used as a preserving solution. After the specimen has been soaked in the formalin solution for a few days the solution should be poured off, the preserved fish wrapped in a damp cloth, rolled in wax paper, or, best of all, plastic sheeting, parcelled, and mailed to:

> Department of Ichthyology and Herpetology
> Royal Ontario Museum
> 100 Queen's Park
> Toronto, Ontario M5S 2C6

A label giving the place and date of collection, together with the name and address of the sender, should accompany the parcel.

INTRODUCTION TO SECOND EDITION

MANY CHANGES in the lakes and streams of eastern Canada have occurred since this book was first published in 1954. These changes involve increasing pollution, the installation of hydroelectric dams, and watershed diversions, to mention only a few. Doubtless in the years to come, more drastic changes will be made, always in the guise of progress. Nowhere, however, have these changes been so striking as in the Great Lakes.

The fish fauna of the Great Lakes has been completely altered in a decade. The famous fishery on Lake Erie for blue pike, whitefish, and cisco is gone. Trawlers now fish smelt and yellow perch are taken by other methods. The blue walleye, unique to lakes Erie and Ontario, is apparently extinct. The sea lamprey has destroyed the lake trout populations of all but Lake Superior, and even here the issue is still in doubt. The removal of the predaceous lake trout seemed to set off a chain reaction among the cisco populations, which apparently hybridized extensively and changed in form and habits. Some species seem to have disappeared entirely.

The fauna has also been altered by the invasion of species other than the sea lamprey. The white perch was unknown in the Great Lakes until about 1952, but by 1964 had become the dominant species in many parts of Lake Ontario. The alewife has now become firmly established in Lake Huron and has invaded Lake Superior, where its numbers are increasing. The gizzard shad and the white bass are also extending their ranges to the upper Great Lakes. In the inland waters the smelt has become established in many lakes in the Muskoka district and, even more unfortunately, it has finally become established in Lake Simcoe. Large scale introductions of kokanee and other species by management agencies, if successful, will undoubtedly trigger further changes.

The changes in Quebec and the Maritime Provinces are less drastic and less apparent than in the Great Lakes, which suffer mainly from an ever-increasing pollution load imposed by a rapidly growing human population. But the Great Lakes pollution load passes through Quebec on its way to the sea and in so doing leaves its mark. The construction of generating plants, steel mills, and other industrial water users in various parts of the Maritime Provinces, Newfoundland, Quebec, and Ontario will produce further changes, as yet unrecorded. For a nation that courts tourist dollars with such undisguised relish, we are surprisingly blind to the continuing destruction of our one unique tourist attraction—an abundance of clean water, our lakes and rivers.

This edition is dedicated
to the memory of J. R. Dymond.

AUTHOR'S COMMENTS, 1974

SINCE PUBLICATION of the 1967 edition much advance has been made in the knowledge of the fishes of our region. Also, some name changes have been suggested in the 1970 revision of the *List of Common and Scientific Names of Fishes*, published by the American Fisheries Society (hereafter referred to as "AFS list"). The more important of these changes and additions follow:

Lepisosteus osseus has been reported from Nipigon Bay, Lake Superior.

Oncorhynchus masou Brevoort, the CHERRY SALMON, has been planted in Westward Lake, Algonquin Park, Ontario. See account by W. J. Christie in Copeia, 1970 (2): 378–379.

Salvelinus alpinus has been discovered in Portage Lake, Restigouche County, N.B.

Coregonus clupeaformis is now known to occur in Mountain Lake, Kijimkujik National Park, Nova Scotia.

The SHALLOWWATER CISCO becomes the CISCO or LAKE HERRING in the AFS list.

Coregonus kiyi occurs in lakes Huron and Michigan.

Coregonus reighardi occurs in lakes Huron and Michigan.

The AMERICAN SMELT becomes the RAINBOW SMELT in the AFS list. It now occurs in Eva Lake, Rainy River District of Ontario.

Esox lucius does not occur in New Brunswick.

The QUILLBACK CARPSUCKER becomes the QUILLBACK in the AFS list.

The HOG SUCKER becomes the NORTHERN HOG SUCKER in AFS list.

The NORTHERN REDHORSE becomes the SHORTHEAD REDHORSE in the AFS list.

Moxostoma carinatum has been reported from Mississippi River, Lanark County, Ontario.

Semotilus corporalis has been recorded from Nova Scotia.

Semotilus margarita has been recorded from the Churchill River, Labrador.

Campostoma anomalum, the STONEROLLER, is now known to occur in southwestern Ontario.

Chrosomus eos is known to occur on Prince Edward Island, probably by introduction. The common name becomes NORTHERN REDBELLY DACE. The AFS list also suggests that the genus *Chrosomus* be abandoned in favour of *Phoxinus* for both *eos* and *neogaeus*, but this opinion is not accepted here.

Notropis cornutus occurs northward in Ontario at least to Duff Twp., near Cochrane, and Lake Temiskaming (not Lake Abitibi).

Notropis photogenis, the SILVER SHINER, is now known to occur in southwestern Ontario.

Opsopoeodus emiliae Hay becomes *Notropis emiliae* (Hay).

Hybopsis biguttata (Kirtland) again becomes *Nocomis biguttatus* (Kirtland).

Hybopsis micropogon (Cope) again becomes *Nocomis micropogon* (Cope).

The BRIDLED SHINER becomes the BRIDLE SHINER in the AFS list.

The CUTLIPS becomes the CUTLIPS MINNOW in the AFS list.

Noturus insignis, the MARGINED MADTOM, has been reported from southwestern Quebec (1974).

Anguilla rostrata has been caught in eastern U.S. waters of Lake Superior.

Fundulus notatus, the BLACKSTRIPE TOPMINNOW, is now known to occur in southwestern Ontario.

Culaea inconstans—a single specimen has been recorded from Nova Scotia.

Gasterosteus aculeatus has long been known to occur in the coastal waters of Hudson and James bays.

The family Serranidae has been more precisely defined and the name Serranidae is replaced by Percichthyidae, now called the TEMPERATE BASSES. This change also applies to the key, page 122, couplet 28. Also, the genus *Roccus* is replaced by the genus *Morone* for all three species, which are now called *Morone saxatilis* (Walbaum), *Morone chrysops* (Rafinesque), and *Morone americana* (Gmelin).

The BLUEGILL occurs in Lake Huron drainage.

The YELLOWBELLY SUNFISH becomes the REDBREAST SUNFISH in the AFS list.

Percina shumardi has the cheek and opercle scaled rather than as noted on page 104.

The SAND DARTER becomes the EASTERN SAND DARTER in the AFS list.

Etheostoma nigrum does NOT occur in New Brunswick.

Etheostoma caeruleum—the reported occurrence in the St. Lawrence River drainage of Quebec is in doubt.

Cottus bairdi is not known to occur in New Brunswick but does occur in Quebec.

Cottus cognatus is not known to occur in Nova Scotia.

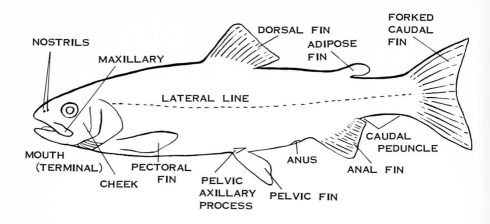

HYPOTHETICAL FISHES SHOWING EXTERNAL PARTS

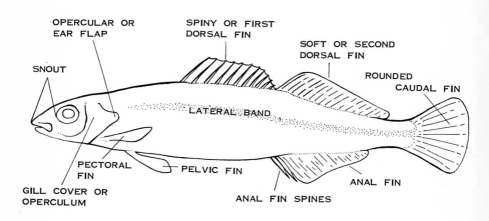

ARRAY OF FISHES

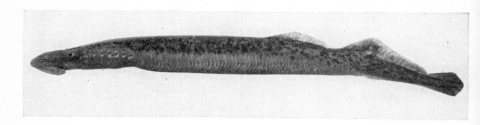

SEA LAMPREY
Petromyzon marinus Linnaeus

Other common names: Marine lamprey, lamprey, lamper eel, lamper, bloodsucker, lamproie de mer.

Distinguishing features: The sea lamprey can be easily distinguished from the "true" fishes by the features characteristic of the lamprey family: the absence of jaws and paired fins, and the presence of seven pores along each side of the body. This lamprey may be distinguished from the three other species of lampreys found in the region by the large diameter of the circular mouth, which is lined with horny teeth radiating from its centre, and by the presence of two distinct dorsal fins. Many of the teeth of the innermost row are bicuspid. The adult sea lamprey is considerably larger than the other three species, which will also assist in its identification. The larvae are blue-gray in colour and lack the teeth and large mouth of the adult. They have a hood-like structure extending over the mouth and the eyes are imperfectly developed. The adult sea lamprey is slate-blue in colour, speckled with deeper blue or black on the back and sides, shading to gray below. Trunk myomeres 67–74.

Size: The sea lamprey may attain a length of 30 inches or more but the average size is 15 to 18 inches. Newly transformed sea lampreys are 6 to 8 inches in length.

Occurrence: The sea lamprey is primarily an Atlantic coastal species and in the Maritime Provinces and Quebec enters fresh water streams flowing into the sea or into the Gulf of St. Lawrence. It invaded the St. Lawrence River and Lake Ontario, but was apparently prevented from reaching the upper Great Lakes by the Niagara Falls. This obstruction was removed with the construction of the Welland Canal, and the sea lamprey is thought to have gained access to the upper Great Lakes by means of this channel. It is now firmly established in all of the Great Lakes. The population in Lake Ontario is native to the lake, frequently said to be landlocked.* It occurs in some inland lakes in the Tobique River System, N.B., probably a permanent resident.

Life history and habits: In the Great Lakes this lamprey ascends streams to spawn in the spring, usually in May. The spawning fish excavate a shallow depression in the gravelly or stony bottom, where the water is shallow and swiftly flowing. The parent fish pick up small stones with their sucking mouths and drift downstream a few feet before releasing them. They thus form a depression in the bottom and at the same time build up a parapet-like structure at the downstream edge of the depression, which serves to restrict the flow of water over the nest. The eggs and sperm are released

---

*Such populations of marine fishes, dwelling permanently in fresh water, are frequently said to be "landlocked." This is not always so, however, for in some cases the species has open access to the sea if it wished to return and, hence, is not prevented by land connections.

and settle among the stones in the depression, or nest. After spawning, the parents move downstream and die. On hatching, the larval lampreys drift downstream and establish themselves in the soft mud under less rapidly flowing water. Here they remain for 4 or 5 years feeding on microscopic animals (plankton) and other material which they strain out of the water and mud. They then develop the funnel-like mouth, lined with teeth, and move downstream to the lake, where they commence the parasitic phase of their lives. They remain in the lake for one or two years, feeding on fishes, until they attain maturity and begin spawning activity.

Food: The adult sea lamprey feeds on the blood and flesh of fish. These it obtains by attaching itself to the fish's body with its suction-cup mouth and rasping a hole through the body covering. The blood and flesh thus exposed are sucked into the digestive tract. Often the attacked fish will live and suffer further attacks, but in many cases the wound is so severe that the host dies. Lake whitefish, lake trout, suckers, ciscoes, and burbot are among the principal species on which the sea lamprey feeds.

Comments: The sea lamprey is considered to be a serious menace to the Great Lakes' fisheries. The decline of the lake trout fishery in Lake Huron is attributed to the tremendous increase in abundance of this lamprey. Government agencies in Canada and in the United States are engaged in methods to control its numbers. Large numbers were caught in the spring in weirs erected at stream mouths but selective poisoning of larvae in natal streams is more effective and is the major control method now in use. Processed lamprey (smoked and/or salted) is said to be quite palatable. In some regions, notably in Quebec, the larvae are used as live bait.

THE LAMPREYS   family PETROMYZONTIDAE

The lampreys are not typical fishes and are easily distinguished from "true" fishes since they lack so many of the typical fish-like characteristics. They do not have true jaws; instead the mouth is a circular funnel-shaped opening; they do not have paired fins (pelvic and pectoral fins); instead of a gill cover they have seven pore-like openings along each side of the body immediately behind the head; the body has a covering of smooth, slippery skin in place of scales. Although popularly called "lamper eels" because of their eel-like shape, this name is misleading since they are not related to the true eels. There are four species of lampreys in the region, of which two are parasitic on fishes and two are not. The adults of the four species of lampreys are easily distinguished from each other by their external features. The larvae, on the other hand, require considerable study before the species can be determined.

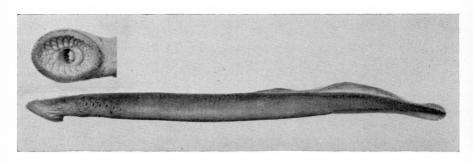

SILVER LAMPREY
Ichthyomyzon unicuspis Hubbs and Trautman

Other common names: Northern lamprey, lamper, lamper eel, lamproie argentée.

Distinguishing features: The silver lamprey resembles the other species of lamprey, lacking jaws and paired fins, and having seven pores along each side. Like the sea lamprey, the silver lamprey has a large, funnel-like mouth. The diameter of the mouth, when expanded, is greater than that of the body, a feature distinguishing it from the northern and American brook lampreys. The mouth is lined with sharp, horny teeth which radiate outward from the centre. The innermost ring of teeth are unicuspid. It may be distinguished from the sea lamprey by the long, continuous dorsal fin (the sea lamprey has two, distinctly separated, dorsal fins). The body is silvery or silvery-blue (sometimes brown) in colour, shading to light silvery below. Trunk myomeres 47–55.

Size: This lamprey attains a length of about 12 inches.

Occurrence: The silver lamprey occurs in the upper St. Lawrence River drainage, and in Lake Champlain. It is rare in Lake Ontario but is found in the remaining Great Lakes, Lake of the Woods, Lake Nipissing, and their tributaries.

Life history and habits: The silver lamprey inhabits lakes and large rivers. Its spawning habits are essentially the same as those of the sea lamprey. The spawning fish ascend streams in the spring, build a nest, spawn, and die. The young burrow into the mud, where they remain for several years. Final development from larval to adult form takes place in the spring. The young adults then move downstream to a larger body of water and commence their parasitic existence. Recent studies indicate that the free-swimming adults live only one year as parasites, then attain sexual maturity, spawn, and die.

Food: The silver lamprey obtains its food in the same manner as the sea lamprey. It attacks almost all species of fish but especially lake whitefish, lake trout, suckers, and catfishes.

Comments: The silver lamprey has not reached the abundance attained by the sea lamprey and is not as destructive as that species. Because of its smaller size, the wounds inflicted by this species are smaller than those caused by the sea lamprey.

AMERICAN BROOK LAMPREY
Lampetra lamottei (LeSueur)

Other common names: Brook lamprey, lamper, lamper eel, lamproie américaine de ruisseau.

Distinguishing features: This non-parasitic lamprey is similar in general appearance to the silver lamprey and the sea lamprey. It may be distinguished from the larger, parasitic lampreys by the weakly developed teeth, which are arranged in groups and not in radiating series. The smaller size of the body and the small mouth will further distinguish it from the sea lamprey. There are two distinct dorsal fins, separated by a distinct notch (unlike the silver and northern brook lampreys). It is a blue-gray colour above, becoming light gray on the sides and light below. Trunk myomeres 64–70.

Size: This species ranges from 5½ to 7 inches in length.

Occurrence: The American brook lamprey occurs in streams in the St. Lawrence drainage of southern Quebec and, in Ontario, in streams flowing into western Lake Ontario, Lake Erie, Lake Huron, and Lake Superior.

Life history and habits: This lamprey inhabits clear streams, often those in which sculpins and brook trout occur. Spawning usually takes place in May in shallow, gravelly riffles. Frequently, large numbers of adults may gather in one particular section of the stream. Like the sea lamprey, the adults excavate a shallow depression in the gravel and deposit the eggs and sperm. The young, on hatching, drift downstream and burrow into a soft mud bottom, where they remain for 4 or 5 years. Final development from larval to adult form takes place and the adults emerge from the bottom ooze in the fall of the year. They over-winter without food, for their digestive tracts are degenerate and non-functional, spawn the following spring, and die.

Food: The adults do not eat. The larvae feed on small microscopic plants and animals which they extract from the water and mud.

Comments: The American brook lamprey is occasionally used as live bait, particularly in Quebec. It is probably most frequently observed during spring spawning activities.

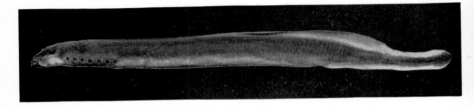

NORTHERN BROOK LAMPREY
Ichthyomyzon fossor Reighard and Cummins

Other common names: Michigan brook lamprey, brook lamprey, lamproie de ruisseau du nord.

Distinguishing features: This small, non-parasitic lamprey is similar in general appearance to the other species of lamprey. A characteristic distinguishing this species from the silver and sea lamprey is the small mouth, less in diameter, when expanded, than the body. The teeth are very weak and degenerate. The single dorsal fin is continuous with the caudal fin, a feature which separates this species from the American brook and the sea lampreys. The back and sides of the northern brook lamprey are gray or brown in colour, shading to silver gray on the under surface. Ripe females may have an orange tint on the "throat." Trunk myomeres 51–58.

Size: The adults attain a length of 5 to 6 inches.

Occurrence: The northern brook lamprey occurs in the St. Lawrence and Great Lakes drainage of Quebec and Ontario. It has been reported to occur in the Yamaska River, which flows into the St. Lawrence River at Sorel, Quebec. In Ontario it is found in streams of the Thames River system in the counties of Kent, Middlesex, and Elgin. It also occurs in streams in Grey County in the vicinity of Owen Sound, in Lake Nipissing, and in some rivers on the north shore of Lake Superior, such as the Chippawa, Pays Plat, and McIntyre. Although it is not a common species in Ontario, it is possible that it has been overlooked by collectors because of its small size and brief adult existence.

Life history and habits: This lamprey is a stream dweller. Spawning takes place in May or June on gravelly riffles in streams, after which the adults die. As in the case of the other lampreys, the young larvae settle down into the bottom mud, where they remain for 6 or 7 years. Like the American brook lamprey, the adults emerge in the fall of the year and, after spending the winter in the stream without food, they spawn and die. Feeding is impossible because the digestive tract is non-functional.

Food: Small microscopic animals and plants are eaten in the larval stage, but the adults do not eat.

Comments: It is reported that the larval form of this lamprey is a popular live bait in some parts of Quebec.

LAKE STURGEON
Acipenser fulvescens Rafinesque

Other common names: Rock sturgeon, sturgeon, esturgeon de lac.

Distinguishing features: The lake sturgeon has an elongate, almost cylindrical body, which tapers toward the head and tail. The snout is long and pointed. The toothless mouth is situated beneath the head. On the underside of the head, halfway between the tip of the snout and the upper lip of the mouth, is a row of 4 barbels. The upper lobe of the caudal fin is larger and more developed than the lower lobe. There are 5 horizontal rows of heavy, bony plates along the body. The bony plates on young fish have sharp, elongated spines, but become smooth and partly embedded in adults. The coloration of the lake sturgeon changes with size. Young fish are usually buff or reddish, often with dark blotches of slate gray or black on the sides. The slate-gray colour predominates on older fish. Large lake sturgeon are usually dark gray, dark green, or black and have a smooth skin.

Size: In the Great Lakes, lake sturgeon approaching 300 pounds in weight, and 7 feet in length were formerly caught. Such large fish are now of rare occurrence although a male fish weighing 220 pounds, caught in Lake Erie, was examined by the author in 1948. In inland lakes the fish are smaller and seldom exceed 100 pounds in weight.

Occurrence: This fish occurs in the upper St. Lawrence River and Lake Champlain, in all the Great Lakes, and in Lake of the Woods. Inland, in Ontario and Quebec, it is found in the large lakes and rivers northward to Hudson Bay. Except in some of these northern lakes, the lake sturgeon is not nearly as common as in former years.

Life history and habits: The lake sturgeon is a bottom living fish of the shallow waters of lakes and large rivers. Spawning occurs in the spring or early summer at temperatures of 55 to 60°F. It may ascend streams for this purpose or spawn in the shallow water of lakes. The lake sturgeon is a slow growing and long-lived fish, many years being required for it to reach maturity. It is known to reach an age of 50 years in Ontario and Quebec. At this age it may be about 5 feet long. At an age of approximately 20 years, it attains a length of 40 inches and a weight of 15 to 20 pounds (upper St. Lawrence River).

Food: The lake sturgeon is a bottom feeding fish. Using its large mouth, which can be extended tube-like, it sucks up quantities of bottom material from which the edible portions are separated. The 4 barbels in front of the mouth are sensitive and assist the fish in locating its food. The principal organisms eaten are molluscs (snails and small clams), aquatic insect larvae (especially of mayflies, caddis flies, and midges), crayfish, small amounts of fish, and aquatic vegetation.

Comments: In the early pioneering days in Canada, the lake sturgeon, which occurred in numbers, was considered a nuisance by fishermen in whose nets it became entangled. Tons were brought ashore and destroyed, the flesh being considered unfit for food. This attitude changed, of course, when it was realized that both flesh and eggs (from which caviar is made) were flavorous and readily marketable. Because of its slow growth, populations of this fish can be quickly wiped out by commercial fishing, and so commercial sturgeon fisheries must be carefully regulated by government agencies. It is caught commercially in pound nets, in large mesh gill nets, or on large baited hooks, set on the bottom. Lake sturgeon command a high market price. Most of the lake sturgeon caught in Ontario are exported to the United States. For further details see Harkness, W. J. K. and J. R. Dymond, The Lake Sturgeon, Ontario Dept. Lands and Forests, 121 pp., 1961.

THE STURGEONS   family ACIPENSERIDAE

Twenty-five species of sturgeons are known in the world, some species living in the rivers and lakes of each of North America, Europe, and Asia. Seven species occur in North America. Sturgeons are primitive fishes for, although as a group they were much more numerous 100 million years ago, fossil evidence indicates that living species differ but little from their ancient ancestors. Characteristic features of all sturgeons are the five rows of bony plates, the asymmetrical or shark-like tail fin, the toothless inferior mouth preceded by four tactile barbels, the cellular swim bladder, and the cartilaginous skeleton.

ATLANTIC STURGEON
Acipenser oxyrhynchus Mitchill

The Atlantic sturgeon, also known as the sea sturgeon, is extremely similar in appearance to the lake sturgeon. The lake sturgeon usually has only one row of bucklers or plates between the anus and the anal fin, while the Atlantic sturgeon has two, three or four rows. In Canada it occurs in the salt waters off the coasts of Quebec, Labrador, and the Maritime Provinces and in the Gulf of St. Lawrence, and in the fresh waters of the St. Lawrence River westward to Montreal. Adults have been known to attain lengths of 6 to 8 feet. In the spring mature fish leave the sea and enter fresh water to spawn. They ascend rivers until they are above the tidal influence before depositing the numerous eggs which may number upwards of 2,000,000 per female. The food of the Atlantic sturgeon consists of mud-dwelling, marine invertebrates and molluscs and, occasionally, fishes. The French name is esturgeon noir.

SHORTNOSE STURGEON
Acipenser brevirostrum LeSueur

In Canada, the shortnose sturgeon is known only from the Saint John River in New Brunswick, although it occurs in inshore marine waters and suitable rivers draining into the Atlantic Ocean, southward to South Carolina. It is the smallest of the North American sturgeons, growing slowly to a length of only 3 feet. It differs from the Atlantic sturgeon in having fewer anal fin rays (19–22 compared with 23–30), more widely spaced dorsal plates, a blackish peritoneum, and smaller size. Although little is known of its life history in New Brunswick waters, elsewhere spawning occurs in the spring. The French name is esturgeon à museau court. For further information see Magnin, E. 1963. Notes sur la repartition, la biologie et particulièrement la croissance de l'*Acipenser brevirostris* LeSueur 1817. Nat. Canadien, 80: 87–96.

THE PADDLEFISHES   family POLYODONTIDAE

Like the closely related sturgeons, the paddlefishes are a primitive group, now reduced to two living species, one in China and one in North America.

PADDLEFISH
Polyodon spathula (Walbaum)

Distinguishing features: The body of the paddlefish is robust and thickset. The skin is smooth and scaleless. It has a greatly elongated, spatula-like snout and the mouth is large and toothless. The pointed gill covers are greatly elongated and extend far back on the sides. It is gray or blue-gray on the back, shading to light gray below.

Size: In the United States this fish may weigh up to 40 pounds and, occasionally, it has been reported to attain a weight of 150 pounds.

Occurrence: The paddlefish is characteristic of the waters of the Mississippi River system but it has been reported to occur, in past years, in the Ontario waters of the Great Lakes. The records of its occurrence are as follows: in Lake Erie, Lake Huron near Sarnia, Spanish River on Georgian Bay, and Lake Helen on the Nipigon River. The paddlefish has not been recorded from any Ontario waters for over 50 years.

Life history and habits: Spawning apparently takes place in late winter or early spring, but knowledge of its spawning habits is incomplete. It inhabits mud-bottomed lakes or large rivers.

Food: The food is reported to consist of crustaceans and other plankton, and aquatic insects.

Comments: The flesh of the paddlefish is excellent and the eggs, when processed, produce good quality caviar. The fish is now of rare occurrence in the northern parts of its range.

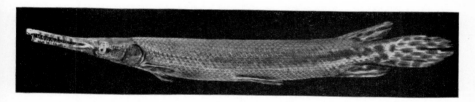

SPOTTED GAR
Lepisosteus oculatus (Winchell)

Other common names: Shortnose gar, billfish.

Distinguishing features: The spotted gar is very similar to the more common longnose gar. It has the long, cylindrical body, the hard, diamond-shaped scales, and the beak-like mouth characteristic of the gar family. It may be distinguished from the longnose gar by its shorter "beak," which is only about 5 to 10 times as long as its narrowest width. There are large, round, black spots on the top of the head and "beak" which are absent on the longnose gar. The back is olive-green in colour, becoming gray-green on the sides and gray below.

Size: The estimated average length in Ontario waters is 2 feet.

Occurrence: In Ontario this fish has been captured in the shallow, weedy waters of Lake Erie, such as those of Long Point Bay. More recently it has been caught in the Detroit River and Lake St. Clair. Essentially a southern species, the spotted gar occurs southward in the United States to Texas.

Life history and habits: The spotted gar is found in shallow, weedy bays. Spawning occurs in the spring of the year in the shallow water, among aquatic vegetation.

Food: The food consists almost entirely of fish. Perch and minnows form a large part of the diet.

Comments: The spotted gar is of no value as a game or commercial species. Because of its rare occurrence in our waters, it is not as well known as the longnose gar.

THE GARS

family LEPISOSTEIDAE

In general the gars are southern fishes and at least four species inhabit the southern and central United States. The scales are hard, diamond-shaped plates of bone which, by interlocking, provide a tough armour-like covering. They are long, cigar-shaped fishes with a prolonged beak-like snout which has a marginal lining of strong, pointed teeth. Although possessing gills, the gar frequently rises to the surface to expel air from the air bladder and take in a fresh supply. This ability to use atmospheric air allows the gar to live in waters of low oxygen content. Small gars may be easily kept in aquaria but they require live food.

LONGNOSE GAR
Lepisosteus osseus (Linnaeus)

Other common names: Gar pike, common garpike, gar, billfish, lépisosté osseux.

Distinguishing features: The body of the longnose gar is greatly elongated and almost cylindrical. It is covered with hard, thick, diamond-shaped scales or plates, which meet (and interlock) but do not overlap. The snout and lower jaw are drawn out to form a long, narrow, beak-like mouth. On the jaws are long, sharp, needle-like teeth. The "beak" is about 15 to 20 times as long as its narrowest width. The dorsal fin is placed far back, nearer the tail than the head. The body is more colourful than that of the spotted gar. The back is dark green shading to pale green or silvery on the sides and white below. Caudal, anal, and dorsal fins are yellow in colour, with dark green or black blotches.

Size: This species commonly grows to a length of 3 feet and, occasionally, to 4 feet.

Occurrence: The longnose gar occurs from the St. Lawrence River below Quebec City, southeastward to Lake Ontario, Lake Erie, Lake St. Clair, Lake Huron, and Georgian Bay. It also occurs in the Ottawa River, Lake Simcoe, and connecting waters to Georgian Bay and Lake Nipissing. Like the spotted gar, it is a fish of southern waters, occurring southward in the United States to Mexico.

Life history and habits: The longnose gar is found in shallow, weedy bays and back-waters. Adults and young may often be seen lying motionless just below the surface of the water in wait for their prey. Spawning takes place in the spring, in May and June, in shallow water among aquatic vegetation or on gravelly or stony shoals.

Food: The food of the longnose gar consists almost entirely of fish, and includes yellow perch, minnows, sunfishes, and other game and forage fishes. The food is digested rapidly and gars caught in nets left in the water more than a few hours usually have empty stomachs.

Comments: The longnose gar is a predacious fish of no known value as a commercial or game species. It is a nuisance to commercial fishermen, becoming ensnarled in their nets by means of the long, needle-like teeth. It is seldom caught by anglers.

BOWFIN
Amia calva Linnaeus

Other common names: Dogfish, freshwater dogfish, mudfish, grindle, beaverfish, amie.

Distinguishing features: The body of the bowfin is robust and almost cylindrical in cross-section. The head and mouth are large, the latter possessing strong, sharp teeth. On the lower surface of the head, in the angle of the lower jaws, is a hard, bony plate called the gular plate which, among our freshwater fishes, is found only on the bowfin. Nostril barbels are prominent. Males have a prominent black spot with a yellow border on the upper part of the base of the rounded caudal fin. On females the yellow border, and often the spot itself, is absent. The colour on the back is dark green, with irregular dark blotches or bars on the flanks; large fish are frequently brownish-green on the back, shading to cream or yellow below.

Size: Few accurate weights are available but Georgian Bay specimens may attain weights of 10 or 11 pounds. The average size is estimated to be 2 to 3 pounds.

Occurrence: The bowfin occurs in the upper St. Lawrence River, the Ottawa River, Lake Champlain and throughout the Great Lakes (excepting Lake Superior) to Sault Ste. Marie. It also occurs in some inland lakes in Ontario, such as Lake Nipissing and Lake Simcoe.

Life history and habits: The bowfin inhabits the shallow waters of warm, weedy bays, inlets and lagoons. Spawning takes place in the spring in shallow water. The male shapes a circular nest among the weeds in which the female lays her eggs. He then guards the eggs and later the young until the latter are an inch or more in length. Like the gars, the bowfin can make use of atmospheric oxygen by taking gulps of air at the surface of the water.

Food: The bowfin is a carnivorous fish, feeding mostly on other fishes. Crayfish are also eaten in quantity.

Comments: The bowfin is often caught on hook and line and is frequently captured in commercial seines, especially in Lake Erie. The flesh, however, is soft and jelly-like; hence, it is not important as a game or commercial species except in cases where live fish are desired for market.

THE BOWFINS   family AMIIDAE

Only in North America is there a living representative of this family of primitive fishes that flourished millions of years ago, according to the fossil evidence in Europe and North America. The one living species is of interest because it possesses such unique characters as a cellular air bladder that assists in respiration, a type of spiral valve in the intestine, and a gular plate on the lower jaw.

AMERICAN SHAD
Alosa sapidissima (Wilson)

Other common names: Shad, alose d'Amérique.

Distinguishing features: This fish is deep-bodied and strongly laterally compressed. There are very weak teeth present on the jaws. The midline of the belly is compressed to knife-edge thinness and is sharply and strongly saw-toothed. The anal fin has a long base and 30 to 32 close-cropped fin rays. The lower jaw, unlike that of the alewife, does not project but fits into a notch in the upper jaw when the mouth is closed. In addition, the silvery cheek is deeper than it is wide. The maxillary bone extends behind the eye. The back is blue or blue-green in colour and the sides are bright silvery.

Size: The average length of this fish is 15 to 18 inches, but it may reach a length of 2 feet.

Occurrence: The American shad is a marine fish, which ascends fresh water streams of the Maritime Provinces and Quebec and, occasionally, of Newfoundland. An annual "run" of American shad occurs in the Ottawa River, north to Point Fortune. It does not occur in any other Ontario waters.

Life history and habits: This is a marine species which spawns in fresh water. In the spring it enters rivers, depositing its eggs in the shallow upper regions. It is not known whether the fish which spawn in the Ottawa River are permanent fresh water residents or come from the sea.

Food: The food of the American shad consists principally of marine plankton.

Comments: The white, flaky flesh of the American shad is highly esteemed. Its eggs, when prepared, are sold as caviar.

THE HERRINGS   family CLUPEIDAE

The herrings are laterally compressed, silvery fishes which occur in large numbers in salt water. Some species, such as those considered on the following pages, also occur in fresh water. Many members of the family have the belly compressed to knife-edge thinness and the scales along this edge form a sharp, saw-toothed margin. The jaws lack strong teeth. The adipose fin, which is found on the whitefishes and salmon-like fishes, is absent. The Atlantic and Pacific herring, the shad, and the true sardines are marine members of this family.

A L E W I F E
Alosa pseudoharengus (Wilson)

Other common names: Gaspereau, sawbelly, shad, "crazy fish," gaspareau.

Distinguishing features: The alewife has a moderately deep body and is strongly compressed laterally. The belly is compressed to knife-edge thinness and strongly scuted with specialized scales, giving it a sharp, saw-toothed appearance. The anal fin has a long base and 16 to 20 short, close-cropped fin rays. The alewife is distinguished from the American shad by its projecting lower jaw and the silvery cheek which is longer than deep. The maxillary bone extends to under the eye. The back is green or brownish-green (dark blue after death) in colour, shading to bright silvery on the sides and belly. A dark spot is often evident immediately behind the head.

Size: The average length of the alewife in Lake Ontario and Lake Erie is about 6 inches. In salt water the average length is approximately 10 inches.

Occurrence: The alewife is primarily a marine fish and occurs in the Atlantic coastal waters, ascending fresh water streams in the spring. In fresh water, it is found in the Maritime Provinces, the St. Lawrence River drainage of Quebec, (Lac St. Louis), Lake Ontario, Lake Erie, Lake St. Clair, and Lake Huron. It also occurs in some inland lakes in Leeds County (Red Horse, Charleston, Otter, and Beverley) and Frontenac County (Dog and Loughboro), Ontario. Since 1954 it has spread into Lake Superior where its numbers are increasing. Once rare in Lake Huron, it has now become an abundant and sometimes dominant species, as in South Bay, Manitoulin Island.

Life history and habits: In Lake Ontario, the alewife inhabits the open waters. The time of spawning varies and may be late May, June, or July. The spawning fish move into shallow waters and lay their eggs over a sand bottom. Once deposited, the eggs are abandoned by the adults. During the summer months, the alewives often die in large numbers. The dead and decaying bodies cast up on the beach create a great annoyance to cottage owners and bathers. Recent studies indicate that the "die-off" is correlated with changes in water temperature.

Food: Small crustaceans (plankton) and aquatic insects constitute the diet of the alewife.

Comments: In Lake Ontario, where it is abundant, the alewife is the main food of the lake trout. Fresh water alewives are too small for table use but those caught on the Atlantic coast are marketed commercially. The flesh is sweet but bony.

GIZZARD SHAD
Dorosoma cepedianum (LeSueur)

Other common names: Hickory shad, mud shad, lake shad, shad, sawbelly, alose à gésier.

Distinguishing features: The gizzard shad is deep-bodied and strongly compressed laterally. The small mouth which lacks teeth, is slightly overhung by the snout. The belly is compressed to knife-edge thinness, having strong specialized scales (or scutes) projecting along its margin which is sharp and saw-toothed in appearance. The gizzard shad may be distinguished from other members of the family—in fact, from any other fish in the region—by the greatly elongated last ray of the dorsal fin. The small mouth and projecting snout are also distinguishing characteristics. The anal fin has a long base but the rays are short or "close-cropped." The back is blue in colour, shading to silvery on the sides and silvery-white below. There is a dark spot on the "shoulder" (behind the head and above the pectoral fin base), which is prominent in fish up to 6 or 8 inches long. The name "gizzard shad" has arisen because of the thickened muscular wall of the stomach, which resembles the gizzard of a fowl.

Size: The gizzard shad reaches an average length of 9 to 10 inches but, in Lake Erie, it may attain a length of 13 inches.

Occurrence: This fish occurs in the St. Lawrence River and Lake Ontario (rare), in Lake Erie (common), Lake St. Clair, Lake Huron and Georgian Bay. The species has recently extended its range into Lake Superior. In 1961 a 1½-pound specimen was caught in Batchawana Bay in a commercial gill net.

Life history and habits: The gizzard shad frequents mud-bottomed, shallow waters. In the Lake Erie district, the young frequently inhabit river mouths. In late autumn, the adults, too, often assemble in large numbers in shore waters and river mouths. Spawning takes place in shallow water in the spring of the year.

Food: The gizzard shad feeds principally on minute aquatic plants (algae) and other plankton, which it obtains from the bottom mud. Stomachs examined often contain quantities of mud.

Comments: This species is of no importance as a game or commercial fish. It is reported be an important food of some game fishes in waters of the United States. For further information see Miller, R. R., 1960, U.S. Fish and Wildlife Service, Fishery Bulletin 173.

ATLANTIC SALMON
Salmo salar Linnaeus

Other common names: Salmon, landlocked salmon, ouananiche, onnenook, Sebago salmon, saumon atlantique.

Distinguishing features: The body of the Atlantic salmon is elongate and only moderately laterally compressed. The mouth is large with strong teeth on the jaws and tongue. There are only a few weak teeth on the roof of the mouth (on the vomer bone). The maxillary extends to a point just beyond the eye in adults but on immature salmon it extends only to below the eye. The scales are large and obvious. The caudal peduncle is slender. Large black x-shaped, or square, spots occur on the head, including the gill covers, along the body, and on the dorsal and anal fins. The spots do not extend much below the midline of the sides and seldom onto the tail fin. The colour of the body is blue or blue-gray above, becoming silvery on the sides. Males in breeding colour have red blotches on the sides. Young salmon are brown or gray on the back and have 7 to 11 dark vertical bars or parr marks on each side, with red spots situated between the bars. Being dark-spotted, the Atlantic salmon should not be confused with the light-spotted brook and lake trouts. The brown trout has the maxillary extending well beyond the eye, has smaller scales, is brownish in colour and the black spots on the sides have a light halo. The black spots on the rainbow trout are small and numerous, especially on the caudal fin, red spots are absent, and the maxillary extends far behind the eye.

Size: Atlantic salmon which remain throughout their lives in fresh water do not grow to as large a size as those which go to sea. Sea-going salmon average about 5 to 15 pounds in weight, rarely over 30, while those remaining throughout their lives in the fresh waters of Canada are estimated to average about 2 to 3 pounds in weight. A 55-pound fish caught in Grand Cascapedia River, Quebec, may be a Canadian record. The world record, 79 pounds 2 ounces, was caught in Norway.

Occurrence: The Atlantic salmon occurs in the north Atlantic waters and coastal region from Cape Cod northward to Ungava. Permanent fresh water populations occur in Nova Scotia (Grand Lake), New Brunswick (Chamcook Lake), Newfoundland (many lakes), and Quebec (Lake St. John). There was a large freshwater population of Atlantic salmon in Lake Ontario until it commenced to decline about 1835 and was completely extinct by 1890. The planting of Atlantic salmon in Ontario waters commenced as early as 1872. Although numerous plantings have been made since that time, mainly in the waters of Southern Ontario, they have been largely unsuccessful insofar as establishing a permanent population is concerned. However, in Trout Lake, near North Bay, Ontario, an Atlantic salmon population now exists which appears to be successfully maintaining itself.

Life history and habits: The Atlantic salmon is a true anadromous fish; that is, it lives and grows in salt water and returns to fresh water streams to spawn, returning again to salt water. Adult salmon may leave the sea and enter streams in early summer, while others will wait until fall before commencing the upstream migration. Those entering the stream early are more desirable from the angler's point of view because they are available to sportsmen for a greater length of time. Spawning occurs in the late fall—November or December—in the Maritime Provinces. A pair of salmon select and defend an area of the stream, the female constructing a shallow depression (the nest or redd) in the coarse gravel. The eggs are laid, fertilized, and covered with gravel, the finished nest being evident by an elongated pile of gravel. The young salmon on hatching remain in the gravel and live on the nutrients absorbed from the yoke sac. When it is completely absorbed they work out of the gravel and commence to seek their own food. At this stage, and until they leave the stream, they are called "parr" and they have 7 to 11 vertical parr marks on the sides. When 4½ or 5 inches long (usually 2 or 3 years old), the young salmon commence their seaward migration. At this stage they are called "smolts." At the end of their first year in the sea they are known as "grilse." Where the salmon go when at sea is not known, but at any rate they are seldom seen. When mature they return to spawn in streams, often returning to the same stream in which they were hatched. In fresh water the silvery colour is replaced by a dull reddish brown colour. The Atlantic salmon do not all die after the first spawning, but usually spawn a second time. Rare individuals may even return for three or four spawnings. It is known that the Lake Ontario salmon did not go to sea but remained in the lake, ascending streams in the fall of the year to spawn. During the spawning run they were caught in large numbers by the local residents.

Food: In the sea the Atlantic salmon feeds primarily on other fishes, such as herring, capelin, and American smelt. Young salmon in streams eat large numbers of aquatic insects but, upon going to sea, fish soon becomes a major part of their diet.

Comments: The fine game and food qualities of the Atlantic salmon have been esteemed by man for generations and need not be emphasized. The disappearance of the Atlantic salmon from Lake Ontario was a great loss, but one brought about by the features attending civilization rather than the capture of spawning fish. The construction of dams for mills on the spawning streams prevented the fish from reaching the spawning grounds. Deforestation and agricultural activities, combined with pollution, rendered the remaining streams unfit for use by the salmon. An experimental reintroduction of this species into Lake Ontario was conducted in recent years. It indicated that at least one stream was, to a limited exent, suitable for salmon. There are so few suitable spawning streams, however, that re-establishment of a permanent population appears unlikely.

THE SALMONS, TROUTS, CHARS, AND WHITEFISHES
family SALMONIDAE

Members of this family are found in marine and fresh waters of the northern hemisphere, although many species have been introduced into parts of the southern hemisphere. All are dependent upon fresh water for spawning, although many species such as the Atlantic and Pacific salmons may spend many years at sea. The salmons, trouts, and chars have fine scales, well-developed teeth on jaws and tongue and exhibit varying degrees of body coloration, whereas the whitefishes have large scales, teeth are absent or only weakly developed, and the body is silvery in coloration (see key, p. 123. The whitefishes are sometimes regarded as a separate family (Coregonidae). This is probably the most economically important family of freshwater sport and commercial fishes in the world.

PACIFIC SALMONS—genus ONCORHYNCHUS

At various times all five species of Pacific salmon have been introduced, largely unsuccessfully, into the waters of eastern North America. Pacific salmon go to sea during early life and return to their natal stream in two to four years, spawn and die. They are harvested during the initial part of their return journey. As early as 1873 the chinook salmon was introduced into Lake Ontario, while within the last few years efforts have been directed toward the establishment of the kokanee, a freshwater form of the sockeye salmon, *Oncorhynchus nerka*.

PINK SALMON
Oncorhynchus gorbuscha (Walbaum)

In 1956 the Ontario Department of Lands and Forests commenced serious attempts to introduce pink salmon by planting nearly one million eggs, during winter and early spring, in Goose Creek, which flows into southern Hudson Bay. No adult fish returned and the attempt failed. However, a casual planting on June 28, 1956, near Pie Island, Thunder Bay, Lake Superior, of a few hundred fingerlings was much more successful. Two pinks were caught by anglers fishing in Minnesota streams in September, 1959. In 1961 and 1963 more fish were caught. The pink salmon spawns at the end of its second year, indicating that the U.S.-caught fish were the progeny of a successful spawning by the fingerlings planted in 1958. The evidence suggests that more serious attempts to introduce pink salmon might be successful.

In 1958 the Fisheries Research Board of Canada began a programme to introduce the pink salmon into the St. Mary's Bay region of Newfoundland. Between 1958 and 1962 nearly 3,000,000 eggs were planted in the North Harbour River, which flows into the head of the bay. A spawning run of adult pink salmon has not been established.

CHUM SALMON
Oncorhynchus keta (Walbaum)

In January 1955 eggs were planted in a tributary and the main channel of the Winisk River, which flows into Hudson Bay. In May and June fingerling chums were planted in the Attawapiskat River, which empties into James Bay. The introductions were unsuccessful.

COHO SALMON
Oncorhynchus kisutch (Walbaum)

The coho salmon, or coho, also called the silver salmon, is native to the Pacific coast. It was introduced into Lake Erie waters in 1933 but a permanent population was not established. Efforts have been made to re-introduce it into some U.S. and Canadian waters of the Great Lakes with considerable success.

KOKANEE (SOCKEYE SALMON)
Oncorhynchus nerka (Walbaum)

Ontario authorities commenced planting kokanee about 1962. Early results were promising and large numbers of eggs were introduced into lakes Ontario and Huron in 1964-5-6. The recaptures made in the fall of 1966 were promising. The kokanee programme will be followed with great interest.

CHINOOK SALMON
Oncorhynchus tshawytscha (Walbaum)

The chinook, king, spring, tyee, or quinnat salmon is a fish native to the waters of the Pacific coast of North America including those of British Columbia. It is reported to have been introduced into the waters of Lake Ontario as early as 1873 and on numerous occasions thereafter, until the last planting in 1925. As a result of the later plantings, chinook salmon up to 30 pounds in weight were caught and many were reported ascending streams in the fall of the year. However, they never became established and many years have elapsed since the last chinook salmon was captured in Lake Ontario.

BROWN TROUT
Salmo trutta Linnaeus

Other common names: European brown trout, English brown trout, Loch Leven trout, German brown trout, Von Behr's trout, truite brune.

Distinguishing features: The adult brown trout is somewhat laterally compressed and has a thickset or stocky appearance due to the thick caudal peduncle. There are strong teeth on the jaws, tongue, and roof of the large mouth. The maxillary bone extends to a point behind the eye. The caudal fin is square, not forked. The back is brown or olive-brown in colour, shading to lighter brown on the sides and creamy while below. Large black spots (with light borders) are evident on the dorsal fin, the back, and upper portion of the sides—most of the black spots are above the lateral line. There are few or no black spots on the caudal fin. Rusty-red or orange spots, with pale borders, are visible on the sides. The brown trout is easily distinguished from the brook and lake trouts by its black spotting, and from the rainbow trout by its practically unspotted caudal fin. It may be distinguished from the Atlantic salmon by its brown or brownish yellow colouring, smaller scales, longer maxillary bone, the reddish orange or orange colouring on the adipose fin, and the large rust-red or yellow spots on the sides of the adults.

Size: Brown trout weighing up to 14 pounds have been reported from Ontario waters, but the average size caught is much smaller and is estimated to be 12 to 15 inches. A 28½ pound brown was caught in Witless Bay, near St. John's, Newfoundland, in 1962.

Occurrence: This species occurs in North America as a result of extensive introductions, which commenced in the United States in 1883. It was introduced into Canadian waters in Newfoundland in 1884, then into Quebec in 1890, Ontario in 1913, New Brunswick in 1921, and, still later, into Nova Scotia waters. The plantings have since continued and, in most cases, have been successful. Brown trout plantings in southern Ontario have been more successful than those in the more rapidly flowing waters of the north. Some of the Ontario rivers in which brown trout occur are: Humber, Credit, Nottawasaga, Grand, Speed, Sydenham, Saugeen, and Muskoka. In southeastern Newfoundland (Avalon Peninsula) the brown trout is well established and the sea-run populations are expanding.

A native of western Europe, it has been widely introduced into many parts of the world.

Life history and habits: In southern Ontario the brown trout frequents slowly flowing streams or quiet pools rather than rapid waters. It spawns in the fall of the year, often later than the brook trout, in the headwaters of streams. The eggs are laid in shallow depressions made in the gravelly bottom. It has become established in certain waters of Newfoundland, Nova Scotia, New Brunswick, and Ontario. In Europe the brown trout resorts to the sea for part of its life, returning to fresh water to spawn, and its life follows a similar pattern in Newfoundland, where it is established in the coastal waters of the Avalon Peninsula. Growth in Ontario streams is slower than in more southern waters but they attain lengths of 10 inches at two years and 15 inches at age three.

Food: In fresh water the principal food of small brown trout (9 to 12 inches in length) is aquatic and terrestrial insects, while the food of larger specimens (over 13 inches in length) consists largely of fish, especially sculpins (Ontario). Crayfish are eaten regularly by both size groups.

Comments: Although the introduction of this fish into some waters inhabited by brook trout is said to have resulted in the decline of the brook trout, in general the brown trout is considered to be an asset to Ontario waters. It is best suited to waters rendered uninhabitable to brook trout by increased summer temperatures and turbidity due to deforestation and agricultural activities. Populations are often under-utilized as, for example, in Newfoundland where Atlantic salmon receives overwhelming preference.

RAINBOW TROUT
Salmo gairdneri Richardson

Other common names: Steelhead trout, steelhead, coast rainbow trout, silver trout, Kamloops trout, truite arc-en-ciel.

Distinguishing features: The body of the rainbow trout is somewhat laterally compressed (examples over 2 or 3 pounds are often rather deep-bodied). The mouth is large and there are strong teeth on the jaws, tongue, and roof of the mouth. The maxillary bone extends to well behind the eye. There are numerous small black spots on the top of the head, on the body, and on the dorsal, adipose, anal, and caudal fins. The caudal fin is heavily spotted, the spots being arranged in a series of lines radiating, like the rays, from the base of the fin. The posterior half of the gill cover is not as heavily spotted as the remainder of the body. The spots do not extend onto the underparts. There are no red spots on this fish. The rainbow trout derives its name from the vivid red, or reddish purple, broad band which commences immediately behind the eye and extends, as a band, along the side of the body to the caudal fin. It is evident only on mature fish and is especially vivid on breeding males. The back is green, or greenish blue, blending to silvery on the sides and white below. Specimens caught in lakes may be quite silvery and the spots on the body inconspicuous, but those on the caudal fin will be apparent. Smaller fish in streams are characteristically black-spotted.

Size: In general, large size fish are caught in large bodies of water and small fish in streams. Stream-caught rainbow trout are usually under a pound in weight while fish in rivers and lakes are estimated to average 2 to 5 pounds in weight. Sizes up to 18 pounds have been reported from Ontario waters. The Ontario angling record would seem to be an 18-pound, 2-ounce fish caught in Georgian Bay in 1966. Three other rainbows weighing over 15 pounds were reported by the Ontario Federation of Anglers and Hunters Big Fish Contest in 1966. McCrimmon (1956) reports an 18½-pound fish from Lake Simcoe but the method of capture is not noted. In its native waters on the Pacific coast the rainbow trout may weigh 20 pounds or more. A weight of 52¼ pounds has been recorded from British Columbia.

Occurrence: The rainbow trout is native to the waters of the Pacific coast of North America, from California to Alaska. The species has been introduced into many parts of eastern Canada. The planting of rainbow trout in Ontario waters commenced about 1904, when 20,000 eggs were planted in the Sydenham River, Grey County. The Ontario Department of Game and Fisheries began its planting programme in 1918. In Ontario, this trout is permanently resident in Lake Superior, Lake Huron, Georgian Bay, Lake Bernard, Lake Simcoe, and Lake Ontario. Plantings in Nova Scotia have not been successful.

Life history and habits: In early spring, the adults migrate upstream to clear, rapid water and, after the nest is constructed in clean gravel, spawning takes place. The exact time of spawning varies but usually occurs during April or May. After spawning the adults move downstream and resume residence in the lake. Usually, rainbow trout desert the parent stream when 2 or 3 years old (12 inches or less in length) and migrate to lakes where they remain until mature. In Ontario this species is primarily a lake fish and few populations remain permanently in streams or rivers.

Food: The rainbow trout is a carnivorous species, feeding principally in our eastern waters on other fishes, such as yellow perch, lake whitefish, and various species of minnows.

Comments: The rainbow trout is highly regarded as a game fish in Ontario. Quite often, silvery examples caught by anglers during the summer months are reported in local newspapers as "salmon." When in this silvery colour phase, the rainbow is often called a steelhead. The so-called Kamloops trout is not considered a form distinct from the rainbow.

ARCTIC CHAR
Salvelinus alpinus (Linnaeus)

Other common names: Char(r), alpine char, European char, arctic salmon, Hearne's salmon, sea trout, Quebec red trout, Marston's trout, omble chevalier.

Distinguishing features: The arctic char resembles the brook trout in general shape and appearance but differs from it by having a more forked caudal fin; a uniformly coloured back, usually without vermiculations; uniformly dusky dorsal and caudal fins, not dark-barred or vermiculated; and on the sides, large cream or pinkish spots, which do not extend to the back (except in young or small fish). The colour of the back of the arctic char may be olive-green to deep blue, shading to lighter green or blue on the sides (silvery on sea-run forms) and white below. Breeding fish exhibit pronounced red coloration on the sides, underparts, and lower fins. The pectoral and pelvic fins vary in colour from creamy white to pink or orange.

Size: Maximum sizes are not known but sea-run fish are usually larger than those remaining permanently in fresh water. The sea-run (or anadromous) arctic char weigh from 2 to 10 pounds. Fish remaining permanently in fresh water sometimes mature at lengths of 4 and 5 inches. A 20-pound, 5-ounce fish was reported from the Tree River, N.W.T., in 1962, and one estimated to weigh 15.8 pounds was caught in Severn River, Hudson Bay drainage in 1960.

Occurrence: The arctic char occurs in the waters of northern Europe and Asia as well as North America. In North America it occurs in Newfoundland, New Brunswick (reported only recently), Hudson Bay and Hudson Strait drainage in Quebec and Northwest Territories, and westward to Alaska. It also occurs on and about the numerous arctic islands. In August 1960 a 15.8-pound char (a Hudson Bay size record?) was caught in the Severn River, Hudson Bay watershed, Ontario. Two additional specimens, both large, were caught in the Severn and Winisk rivers in 1961 and 1962. It has also been introduced into some inland lakes in Algonquin Park and elsewhere in Ontario.

Life history and habits: The life history of this char in North America is not well known. Spawning takes place in the autumn but the exact time probably varies with the latitude. The mature fish leave the sea and enter fresh water during the summer. Like other members (for example, Atlantic salmon) of the salmon family, the arctic char may remain permanently in fresh water and never go to sea. Such populations are often said to be landlocked.

Food: This char consumes a wide variety of invertebrate marine animals and shrimp-like creatures. Fish also form a large part of its diet, for example, such marine forms as sculpins and sand launces.

Comments: The arctic char is used for food by northern dwelling peoples. It has been rather widely publicized in recent years as a sport fish. An experimental Eskimo-operated fishery was commenced in Frobisher Bay, Baffin Island, in 1958. The char are shipped to eastern Canadian and U.S. markets where they command a high price as a gourmet item. For further information see McPhail, J. D., 1961. Jour. Fisheries Research Board Canada, vol. 18, no. 5, pp. 793–816.

The so-called Marston's trout or the "red trout of Quebec" (omble rouge du Québec), sometimes regarded as a distinct species (*Salvelinus marstoni*) is here considered to be a subspecies of the arctic char. It is confined to Quebec and is characterized by the intense red coloration which suffuses the flanks and underparts of both males and females.

BROOK TROUT
Salvelinus fontinalis (Mitchill)

Other common names: Speckled trout, eastern speckled trout, common brook trout, eastern brook trout, trout, square tail, coaster, mud trout (Newfoundland), Aurora trout, omble de fontaine.

Distinguishing features: The mouth of the brook trout is large with strong teeth on the jaws, tongue, and roof of the mouth. The maxillary extends to a point well behind the eye. The scales are small and very numerous. The caudal fin is characteristically square-cut and not forked. Breeding males develop an upward-curving hook at the forward end of the lower jaw. The coloration of the adult brook trout, although extremely variable, is usually sufficient to distinguish it from all other relatives. The back is greenish to dark brown and, occasionally, almost black; heavy dark wavy lines extend on to the dorsal and caudal fins. On the sides are small but well-defined red spots, bordered by a bluish halo. The leading edge of each lower fin has a pronounced milk-white border. Breeding males become particularly colourful with a strong orange to reddish blush along the lower flanks.

Size: The world record brook trout is a 14¾-pound, 34-inch specimen taken in the Nipigon River, Ontario, in 1915. The usual size in the smaller streams of the southern parts of Ontario is under a pound in weight, but examples of 2 and 3 pounds are not rare in the northern parts of Ontario and Quebec. In 1966 the Ontario Federation of Anglers and Hunters Big Fish Contest listed eight fish over 6 pounds; the largest weighed 9 pounds, 3 ounces. The largest brook trout recorded since the contest began was caught in 1964 and weighed 11 pounds, 3 ounces.

Occurrence: This species is widely distributed in eastern Canada. It occurs in cool, clear streams and lakes from the Maritime Provinces, Newfoundland, and Labrador westward to the Nelson River in Manitoba. It is found from the Great Lakes northward in Ontario to the streams entering Hudson Bay and James Bay. The brook trout has been widely introduced into waters in which it was not native. This is particularly true of the central and western parts of North America.

Life history and habits: In the autumn the mature fish migrate leisurely upstream. In small streams they may sun themselves, resting on submerged logs or rocks for a short time, and then continue their upstream journey. Spawning takes place in late autumn, from late October to early December, in the shallow, gravel-bottomed head waters of streams and occasionally in lakes. The adults construct a shallow depression or redd, in the clean gravel. The redd is usually made by the female. The eggs are deposited and fertilized and then covered with gravel. No other parental care is given and the young, after hatching, live during the winter on the nutrients absorbed from the yolk sac. When the yolk is absorbed, and having freed themselves from the gravel they commence to feed on microscopic organisms.

Food: The brook trout eats a great variety of food, including insect larvae, adult insects, and fish. The slimy sculpin is a common food item of the larger fish.

Comments: The brook trout, because of its beauty, its game qualities, and the cool clean streams and lakes it inhabits, is regarded as one of the finest of game fishes. The flesh, which may be amber, pink, or red in colour, has a delicious flavour. In eastern Canada and the United States, many hatcheries are maintained exclusively for the artificial propagation of this species.

In the 1954 edition, the Aurora trout was listed as a distinct species, S. *timagamiensis* Henn and Rinkenbach, although it was suggested it be regarded as a subspecies. The Aurora is included here with the brook trout, from which it differs in only a few superficial characters. It has become rare indeed, if not extinct, in its native waters of White Pine, Little White Pine, and Whirligig lakes of the Timagami Forest Reserve, Ontario.

LAKE TROUT
Salvelinus namaycush (Walbaum)

Other common names: Common lake trout, Great Lakes trout, gray trout, togue, mackinaw trout, mountain trout, "salmon trout," touladi.

Distinguishing features: The lake trout has an elongate body. The head is large and the snout often projects slightly beyond the lower jaw. The long maxillary extends well behind the eye. There are strong, well-developed teeth on the jaws, tongue, and roof of the mouth. The scales are small. The lake trout may be distinguished by its deeply forked caudal fin and the light-coloured spots on the back, sides, cheeks, gill covers, and dorsal and caudal fins. There are no red spots or other bright colours on the body. The colour varies greatly from lake to lake. In large lakes the back and sides are usually gray or pale green while in small inland lakes this pale coloration is often replaced by dark brown, at times almost black. On the sides, and to a lesser extent on the back, are light-coloured spots, which often run together to form larger spots or worm-like markings. The milk-white leading edges of the lower fins, so prominent on the eastern brook trout, are vague and often absent on the lake trout. The pelvic and pectoral fins sometimes show traces of orange colouring.

Size: The lake trout is one of our largest fresh water fishes. The largest authentic angling record in North America is a 63-pound, 2-ounce fish caught in Lake Superior in 1952. Larger sizes, some in excess of 100 pounds, have been reported from time to time, but few fish weighing over 50 pounds have been reported in recent years. Sizes from 3 to 5 pounds are average in most inland lakes. In 1961 a lake trout, weighing 102 pounds was caught in commercial gill nets set in Lake Athabaska. This is believed to be the maximum size reliably authenticated for North America.

Occurrence: The lake trout is found only in northern North America and occurs nowhere else in the world, except where it has been introduced. In Canada it occurs from the Maritime Provinces and Labrador on the east, to northern British Columbia, Northwest Territories, and the Yukon on the west. The lake trout is found northward in Ontario, in deep lakes, to Hudson Bay, and in Quebec to the Ungava region. Formerly more or less abundant in all of the Great Lakes (always rare in Lake Erie) it is now on the threshold of extinction (except perhaps in Lake Superior), largely as a result of predation by sea lampreys. Although no longer a commercial species, vigorous efforts are being made by Canadian and United States authorities to prevent the complete extinction of this species from Great Lakes waters.

Life history and habits: The lake trout is established only in lakes which, because of their depth, have a large volume of cool, well-oxygenated water, to which the fish can retire during the warm summer months. In the fall of the year as the waters cool the fish leave the deep waters and inhabit waters of more moderate depth. In October or November they seek the shallow waters in which to spawn. Although spawning usually takes place on rocky shoals or reefs, the type of bottom selected varies in different lakes from clay to boulders. The depth also varies from one foot to over 60 feet. Each lake has specific spawning areas which are usually selected year after year. Spawning may also take place in rivers. No attempt is made to guard the eggs. After spawning on the shoals, the fish may retire to deeper water. With the spring break-up of the ice, the lake trout are to be found in the upper or shallow waters until again forced by the rising temperature to seek the cool depths.

Food: The lake trout is carnivorous, feeding principally on other fishes. The ciscoes and the lake whitefish are its principal food in most waters. In Lake Ontario, however the alewife was the species most frequently eaten, while in other lakes, lake whitefish, yellow perch, and American smelt may predominate in its diet. In some inland lakes forage fishes are not present in sufficient quantities or are not available in summer, and the lake trout resorts to plankton and aquatic insects for food. Under such conditions the growth rate is retarded and the size attained is unusually small.

Comments: The lake trout is highly prized both as a game and as a commercial fish. The flesh may be white, pink, or red in colour but, irrespective of its colour, the flavour is usually excellent. An annual average of 2 to 3 million pounds are taken commercially from Ontario waters, while an undetermined number of pounds are captured by sport fishermen. Most of the lake trout taken commercially are captured in gill nets. Deep trolling, by means of a metal line, probably accounts for most of the lake trout caught by sportsmen, but bait casting in the spring of the year, when the fish are in shallow waters, affords the angler more sport. The drastic decline in numbers of lake trout in the Great Lakes and especially Lake Huron and Lake Michigan has resulted from the destructive behaviour of the sea lamprey.

Although many different kinds of lake trout are recognized by fishermen, all belong to this one species. The differences in appearance are mainly due to the different conditions under which they live. The best example is probably the siscowet of the deep waters of Lake Superior, which is pale in colour, deep-bodied, and so fat that it is usually smoked before marketing. The siscowet is sometimes regarded as a subspecies, S. n. siscowet (Agassiz).

For further information see Lindsey, C. C., 1964. Jour. Fisheries Research Board Canada, vol. 21, no. 5.

THE SPLAKE or WENDIGO

If eggs from a female lake trout (S. *namaycush*) are fertilized with sperm from a ripe male brook trout (S. *fontinalis*), the resulting offspring is called a splake or wendigo. It is a fertile hybrid which reproduces in nature and, therefore, presents unlimited possibilities for selective breeding.

This lake trout × brook trout hybrid has received considerable attention from government fishery authorities across Canada, beginning about 1946. Originally heralded as new, this cross or hybrid has been known to fish culturists since 1880, but the work being carried on now in Ontario is new. Serious attempts are being made to selectively breed hybrids with the more desirable qualities of both parents; for example, the deep swimming habit of the lake trout, and the early maturing habits of the brook trout.

The splake grows more quickly than either parent, being about five and ten inches longer, respectively, than brook and lake trout in their fourth year. They are known to live at least nine years and to attain weights of at least 16 pounds. Maturity is reached, on the average, at age three. In some features the hybrids resemble one or the other parent, while in other respects they are intermediate. For example, they tend to spawn during both night and day, although lake trout spawn at night and brook trout during the day. The omnivorous diet, which includes aquatic insects, leeches, and plankton, is similar to that of the brook trout.

The splake has been widely introduced into lakes in Algonquin Park, Algoma, Manitoulin and Sudbury districts, and elsewhere in Ontario and Quebec. It is difficult to identify splake because they are intermediate between the parental types and exhibit great variability. The caudal fin is not as deeply forked as that of the lake trout, but more so than that of the brook trout. The black markings on the dorsal and caudal fins of the brook trout are not evident on splake; these fins are usually light spotted. However, positive identification can usually be made by counting the pyloric caeca, small worm-like appendages on the gut, located just posterior to the stomach; 25–50 for brook trout, 70–80 for splake, and 100–200 for lake trout.

THE WHITEFISHES

Lake whitefish, ciscoes (or "fresh water herring"), and round whitefish are member of the salmon family. They are found in most deep lakes in the northern hemispher and are especially common in the lakes of northern North America, particularly thos of Canada. They are silvery fishes, with large smooth scales. With few exceptions the all lack teeth on the jaws. They possess an adipose fin and an axillary process, or splint of gristle-like material at the base of the pelvic fin. All have soft-rayed fins, in whic sharp spines are absent. The number of rakers on the first gill arch is the most usefu diagnostic character. However, identification of ciscoes to species is most difficult an necessitates consideration of many characters. No satisfactory identification key to specie is available. In the 1954 edition the ciscoes were included in the genus *Leucichthys* bu are here included in the genus *Coregonus*. When members of the whitefish family liv in community with the lake trout, they form its staple food.

The Atlantic whitefish, *Coregonus canadensis*, is a new species only recently described It occurs only in the Tusket River system and Millipsigate Lake in Nova Scotia. Thi whitefish differs from the lake whitefish in a number of characters but especially th terminal mouth, the small scales (91–100 in lateral line compared with 70–85 o lake whitefish), and the presence of small but well-developed teeth on premaxillaries palatines, and vomer.

Heavy exploitation and hydroelectric dam construction have drastically reduced it numbers, especially in the Tusket River system.

LAKE WHITEFISH
Coregonus clupeaformis (Mitchill)

Other common names: Great Lakes whitefish, common whitefish, inland whitefish, whitefish, gizzard fish (N.B.), corégone de lac.

Distinguishing features: The lake whitefish is deep-bodied and laterally compressed. The mouth is overhung by the snout and there are two flaps of skin between the nostrils. On Great Lakes specimens the back is pale greenish-brown in colour becoming silvery on the sides and the fins are light. On specimens from inland waters the back may become dark or black in colour and the fins are heavily speckled with black. Gill raker counts are 22 to 32.

Size: Fifty years ago lake whitefish of over 20 pounds were caught in the Great Lakes, but fish weighing 10 to 15 pounds are now rare and the average is approximately 2 to 4 pounds. In the inland lakes the average weight is one to 3 pounds.

Occurrence: The lake whitefish occurs widely throughout eastern Canada, in New Brunswick, in Quebec and Labrador, and formerly in all of the Great Lakes, and northward in innumerable inland lakes to Hudson Bay. It occurs also on the island of Newfoundland, where it was introduced in 1886.

Life history and habits: In the Great Lakes, lake whitefish spawn in November and December, the females scattering the eggs over rocky, gravelly or sandy shoals. Inland they may ascend streams to spawn. The spawning fish make no attempt to protect the eggs, which hatch during the winter.
The rate of growth in the Great Lakes fish is rapid, especially in the more southern waters where a weight of 2 pounds is reached in 4 to 5 years. They move about in schools and are strong swimmers.

Food: Although adapted to bottom feeding, lake whitefish eat a wide variety of food such as plankton, molluscs (snails), aquatic insect larvae, and occasionally small fishes.

Comments: Once the most valuable commercial species in Ontario, the whitefish of the Great Lakes has been almost destroyed by changing environmental conditions which include pollution and predation by sea lampreys. However, the species continues to support an important Canadian fishery and annually contributes over 20 million pounds (26.5 in 1962) with a landed value of about 4 million dollars. In many inland lakes, it is an important food of the lake trout. It is sought by anglers in winter who fish through the ice, using minnows or jigs for bait. Lake Simcoe is well known among anglers in southern Ontario for its winter whitefish fishery. The flesh is white and flaky, and has an exceptionally fine flavour.

ROUND WHITEFISH
Prosopium cylindraceum (Pallas)

Other common names: Menominee whitefish, frost-fish, pilot fish, bottlefish, ménomini pointu blanc.

Distinguishing features: The long body is slender and rounded as its name implie and thus it differs from the closely related lake whitefish and ciscoes, which are deep bodied and laterally compressed. The mouth, which is small and toothless, is overhung by the snout. There is a single flap of skin between the nostrils. The back is dar blue-green in colour and the sides are silvery. Gill raker counts are 14 to 19. The youn up to 4 inches in length have 3 rows of dark spots along the sides of the body but thes spots are absent in larger young and adults.

Size: The round whitefish is of medium size, averaging approximately a pound i weight but occasional specimens weighing 3 pounds have been reported.

Occurrence: The round whitefish occurs widely throughout eastern Canada, i Labrador, in northern New Brunswick, in Quebec, and from the Great Lakes regio of Ontario to northwestern Canada. In Ontario it inhabits all of the Great Lakes (excep Lake Erie) and Lake Nipigon and has been reported in a few inland lakes.

Life history and habits: The round whitefish frequents the shallow, rather than th very deep, waters of lakes. Spawning takes place in November and December in th mouths of streams and rivers and at times the fish may spawn in the river itself.

Food: Aquatic insects, plankton, and small molluscs (such as snails and small clams) are the main foods.

Comments: The flesh of the round whitefish is white, flaky, and of excellent flavou but the fish is not sufficiently abundant to be of great commercial importance and i seldom, if ever, caught by anglers.

PIGMY WHITEFISH
Coregonus coulteri (Eigenmann and Eigenmann)

Formerly thought to occur only in lakes of northwestern North America, large number of this species were caught in the deeper waters of Lake Superior during experimenta trawling operations by the U.S. Fish and Wildlife Service motor vessel, *Cisco*, in 195 and 1953. The species is widely distributed in Lake Superior in depths ranging from 60 to 300 feet. Studies indicate that greatest abundance occurs from 150 to abou 234 feet.

It may be distinguished from the round whitefish by its small number of pyloric caeca (15–23 compared with 50–116), fewer scales in the lateral line (56–66 compared with 83–96), and its smaller size, seldom over 6 inches in length.

Spawning probably occurs during November and December.

The pigmy whitefish is of no economic importance, but it is of interest that a Great Lakes species could escape detection for such a long time.

SHALLOWWATER CISCO°
Coregonus artedii LeSueur

Other common names: Cisco, common cisco, grayback, blueback, lake herring, shoal-water herring, fresh water herring, tullibee, hareng de lac.

Distinguishing features: The shallowwater cisco is laterally compressed. The mouth s at the front extremity of the head and is not overhung by the snout as in the white-sh. The gill raker count is more than 40. The eyes are large and silvery. The olour of the back varies from dark blue (at times almost black) to a pale gray-reen. The sides are silvery. The pectoral fins are clear, the pelvic and anal fins slightly vhite, but all three fins have traces of black colouring on the tips. The dorsal and audal fins are also clear, but they have a greater concentration of black colouring on heir free margins.

Size: The size varies greatly from lake to lake. In the Great Lakes the largest size vas probably attained in Lake Erie, where specimens weighing 8 pounds have been xamined. The average weight, however, is one-half to one pound. In inland lakes the verage weight is usually under half a pound.

Occurrence: The shallowwater cisco occurs throughout the Great Lakes and in nnumerable inland lakes in Quebec and Ontario, northward to Hudson Bay. They are ommon in many of the deep lakes in southern Ontario, such as Lake Simcoe, Balsam _ake, Lake Nipissing, and many lakes in Haliburton and Victoria counties.

Life history and habits: In November or December the mature fish move into the hallow water near shore and release their eggs and sperm over a sandy or gravelly)ottom. No nest is constructed, the eggs being scattered at random. At other times of he year they are pelagic and move about in schools in the open water. During the ummer months, when the water is warm, they retire to the cooler, deeper waters.

Food: The food of the shallowwater cisco varies with the seasons. The main food is)lankton (small crustaceans and other minute creatures) which is eaten in large juantities throughout the year. In the spring and late autumn, however, when the hallowwater cisco is near the surface, aquatic insects and minnows (such as the :merald shiner) are eaten, particularly by the larger fish.

Comments: The shallowwater cisco is an important commercial species in the Great _akes (currently less abundant and, hence, less important than in past years). It is 1sually the only species of cisco present in the inland lakes and the one most frequently

°The ciscoes (sometimes called fresh water herring or herring) bear a superficial ·esemblance to the true marine herrings, but they are not close relatives of these latter fishes. Nine species of ciscoes occur in the Great Lakes but the shallowwater cisco is the only species considered in detail.

encountered by fishermen. In many inland lakes, the shallowwater cisco serves as an important food of the lake trout. In the spring, in Lake Simcoe, Ontario, it is caught by anglers using artificial flies and live bait; in the winter it is caught through the ice using salted minnows (emerald shiners) for bait. During the fall spawning run in inland lakes, the shallowwater cisco is sometimes captured in quantity by local residents. The flesh has a delicious flavour.

NIPIGON CISCO
Coregonus nipigon (Koelz)

Description: The body of the Nipigon cisco is deep and laterally compressed. The colour has been reported by Dr. J. R. Dymond (*The Fishes of Lake Nipigon,* 1926) as follows: "Colour dark greenish above, silvery on the sides and belly, dorsal and caudal fins tipped with black, lower fins usually with little or no pigment."

Size: The Nipigon cisco is one of the largest ciscoes, reaching a length of over 19 inches.

Occurrence: It is a shallow water species, which occurs in Lake Nipigon, Black Sturgeon Lake, Lake Abitibi, and some small inland lakes in northwestern Ontario. It has also been reported to occur in Quebec.

Comments: The validity of this form as a distinct species is in considerable doubt. It perhaps should be regarded as a deep-bodied form of *C. artedii.*

DEEP WATER CISCOES

The deep water ciscoes or chubs closely resemble the shallowwater cisco in appearance and habits (all are silvery-coloured, plankton-eating fishes). Some of the species are of importance to the commercial fisheries of the Great Lakes, although many of the larger species, notably *C. johannae* and *C. nigripinnis,* have been greatly reduced in numbers by sea lampreys. In Lake Michigan these species no longer exist, and only *C. hoyi* remains. They were frequently smoked for market (smoked herrings) and were in great demand.

SHORTNOSE CISCO
Coregonus reighardi (Koelz)

Description: The shortnose cisco is very similar in appearance to the shortjaw cisco but is less compressed laterally, the head is large, and the lower jaw usually shorter than the upper. The body colour is light green (yellow-green) on the back, shading to silvery on the sides and white below.

Size: It is a commercially important deep water cisco or chub, growing to a length of 14 inches.

Occurrence: This species occurs in Lake Ontario, Lake Superior, and Lake Nipigon in depths varying from 80 to 300 feet.

SHORTJAW CISCO
Coregonus zenithicus (Jordan and Evermann)

Other common names: Shortjaw chub.

Description: The shortjaw cisco has a slender compressed body. The jaws are of about equal length. The body colour is olive-green on the back, blending to silvery on the sides and white below.

Size: It may attain a length of 12 inches and a weight of about one pound.

Occurrence: This species occurs in Lake Huron, Lake Superior, and Lake Nipigon Ontario. It is usually found in deep water to depths of about 200 feet.

Comments: The shortjaw cisco is one of the commercially important deep water scoes or chubs.

LONGJAW CISCO
Coregonus alpenae (Koelz)

Other common names: Longjaw chub.

Description: The longjaw cisco greatly resembles the deepwater cisco in general body shape, coloration, and other features.

Size: The average length is 12 to 14 inches, which is slightly greater than that of the deepwater cisco.

Occurrence: The longjaw cisco occurs in Ontario waters only in Lake Huron, usually depths of 300 to 360 feet. In 1946 and subsequent years specimens were caught in Lake Erie. Originally identified as *Leucichthys johannae*, additional material indicated the species to be *Coregonus (Leucichthys) alpenae*. For further information see Scott, W. B. and S. H. Smith, 1962. Jour. Fisheries Research Board Canada, vol. 19, no. 6, 013–1023.

BLOATER
Coregonus hoyi (Gill)

Other common names: Bloat.

Description: The bloater is a small compressed cisco, in which the lower jaw is usually longer than the upper jaw. (The lower jaw has a hook or protuberance near its tip.) The body is pale green on the back and silvery (with a blue or purplish idescence) on the sides. The fins are generally clear, except for black margins on the dorsal and caudal fins.

Size: The bloater is the smallest of all the ciscoes and reaches a length of 6 to 9 inches.

Occurrence: It inhabits the deep waters of Lake Ontario, Lake Huron, Lake Superior, and Lake Nipigon, in depths ranging from 100 to over 400 feet but is reported to be most abundant at depths of 250 to 300 feet.

Comments: It is a soft, fragile fish. When caught in commercial gill nets, it frequently breaks apart, or, if entire when the nets are pulled to the surface, the abdomen is greatly distended (hence its common name—bloater). Commercially, it is the least important of the ciscoes.

DEEPWATER CISCO
Coregonus johannae (Wagner)

Other common names: Deepwater chub.

Description: The deepwater cisco is a laterally compressed, elongate, silvery species. The lower jaw is generally equal in length to the upper jaw. The colour is pale green above, becoming silvery on the sides and white below.

Size: It attains an average length of 10 to 11 inches.

Occurrence: It is a deep water form, occurring in Ontario waters in Lake Huron, where it is said to reach its maximum abundance at depths of 300 to 450 feet.

KIYI
Coregonus kiyi (Koelz)

Other common names: Chub, waterbelly.

Description: The kiyi greatly resembles the shallowwater cisco. The pectoral, pelvic dorsal, and anal fins are longer than those on the other ciscoes. The lower jaw hooked or has a tubercle projecting beyond the upper jaw.

Size: The average length is approximately 8 to 11 inches.

Occurrence: It occurs only in Lake Ontario and Lake Superior, where it is reported to be uncommon. The kiyi lives at greater depths than the bloater and in Lake Ontario was said to be most abundant at depths of over 400 feet.

Comments: In past years it was of commercial significance in the fisheries of Lake Ontario.

BLACKFIN CISCO
Coregonus nigripinnis (Gill)

Other common names: Blackfin.

Description: The body of the blackfin cisco is generally deep and laterally compressed. The lower jaw usually projects beyond the upper jaw. The body colour is variable from lake to lake—Lake Superior specimens are usually light in colour, while those from Lake Nipigon are dark. The fins are often black in colour, especially toward the tips, showing a marked contrast with the silvery sides.

Size: It is a large species and may reach lengths of over 15 inches.

Occurrence: It occurs in Ontario in Lake Huron, Lake Superior, and Lake Nipigon and has been reported from a few other lakes in the northern portion of the province. The blackfin cisco is primarily a deep water form, inhabiting depths over 300 feet.

ARCTIC GRAYLING
Thymallus arcticus (Pallas)

Although not native to Ontario waters, the grayling did occur naturally in the neighbouring state of Michigan until about 1936. It has been experimentally introduced into some inland lakes in western Ontario by the Department of Lands and Forests. In Great Slave Lake, N.W.T., sizes to 4.1 pounds have been reported.

AMERICAN SMELT
Osmerus mordax (Mitchill)

Other common names: Smelt, freshwater smelt, éperlan d'Amérique.

Distinguishing features: Its slender shape and silvery appearance, the presence of strong teeth on the jaws and especially on the tongue, and the presence of an adipose fin will serve to distinguish the American smelt from our other fishes. The pelvic axillary process, which is present between the pelvic fin and the body of the lake whitefish

sco, salmon, and trout, is absent on the smelt. When caught during the spawning
ns the males feel rough, somewhat like sandpaper, owing to the presence of minute
bercles on the body. At this time the fish have a distinctive odour similar to cucumber.
he scales, which are readily shed, reflect a purple and blue iridescence on freshly
ught fish.

Size: The adults exhibit considerable variation in size in different waters. In Lake
ntario, Lake Erie, and on the east coast, American smelts attain a rather large size
d average 8 to 10 inches in length, but in Lake Huron and Georgian Bay the average
ngth is only 6 to 7 inches. Large American smelts occasionally attain lengths up to
t inches.

Occurrence: The American smelt occurs in rivers and lakes in the Maritime Provinces
d Newfoundland, ascending from the sea to spawn. It is a native species in many
land lakes in New Brunswick (Utopia and Chamcook), Quebec (Champlain, Green,
ac des Isles, Memphremagog, St. John, and others) and eastern Ontario (Muskrat and
olden lakes, Renfrew County). The American smelt now occurs in all of the Great
akes as a result of introductions which commenced in Crystal Lake, Michigan, in 1912.[*]
Ill-advised transport of live smelts by sportsmen has enabled smelts to become estab-
shed in many smaller lakes in the Muskoka District of Ontario. Finally, in 1962, the
melt was reported from Lake Simcoe where its presence cannot be expected to improve
e lake trout and whitefish fisheries. Reports of American smelt in Cameron and
turgeon lakes, Durham County, Ontario, are actually those of the shallowwater cisco,
hich has the habit of forming large schools in certain regions in the spring and fall.

Life history and habits: In the Great Lakes region spawning takes place in early
ring, usually in April, the exact date probably depending on climatic conditions,
pecially temperature. Shortly after nightfall, the spawning fish commence to ascend
reams and freshets, drifting downstream to the lake before daybreak. Occasionally
me of them will remain in a shaded section of the stream during daytime. The spawn-
g run may last for a period of from 10 days to 2 weeks and, in Ontario, is usually
ver before the end of April. In certain areas, notably Lake Erie and the western end
f Lake Ontario, spawning takes place on sandy beaches rather than in streams. Sea-
n American smelt of the east coast move into estuaries in the fall, remain there all
inter, and ascend streams to spawn in the spring.

Food: In the Great Lakes the American smelt feeds on plankton, especially during
e summer months, eating only an occasional fish. Food studies indicate, however,
at a much larger number of fish is eaten during the winter period.

Comments: This fish, whose flesh is of excellent flavour, has become increasingly
opular in Ontario in recent years. It is eagerly sought by fishermen during its spring
pawning runs, at which time it is caught in seines and various types of dip nets. In
ewfoundland, the Maritime Provinces, and more recently in Ontario, it is angled
hrough the ice in winter. In the Maritime Provinces and Ontario the smelt provides a
aluable commercial fishery. In Ontario, annual yields have been as high as 19 million
ounds (1962), mostly from Lake Erie.

HE SMELTS   family OSMERIDAE

The smelts are small, silvery fishes living in the salt (and sometimes fresh) waters
f the northern hemisphere. They are relatives of the salmons, trouts, and whitefishes
ut differ from them in having no pelvic axillary scale. Some are anadromous, entering
resh water to spawn, and such forms may become landlocked (see footnote, page 2).
ll smelts show a tendency to form large schools.

---

[*]It is possible that the Lake Ontario population resulted from plantings made in New
ork State waters or entered by way of the St. Lawrence River.

M O O N E Y E
Hiodon tergisus LeSueur

Other common names: Toothed herring, river whitefish (Ottawa Valley), laquaich argentée.

Distinguishing features: The mooneye is a laterally compressed, deep-bodied, silver fish with large scales. The eyes are large. The mouth is small but there are well developed teeth on the jaws and tongue. The colour of the back is pale green, shading to silvery on the sides. The mooneye bears a close resemblance to the goldeye, but the fleshy keel on the belly does not extend forward beyond the pelvic fins as it does in the goldeye. In addition, the dorsal fin originates in front of the anal fin on the mooneye and behind the front of the anal fin on the goldeye.

Size: The mooneye is approximately the same size as the better-known goldeye averaging 10 to 12 inches in length.

Occurrence: The mooneye occurs in the upper St. Lawrence River and Ottawa River in Lake Ontario, Lake Erie, and Lake St. Clair. It also occurs in the Moose River in northern Ontario and in Lake of the Woods in the western part of the province. Lake Temiskaming records were reported in 1954, and it is now known to occur in a few watersheds of northwestern Quebec.

Life history and habits: This species spawns in the spring of the year. It is thought to ascend rivers and streams and spawn in shallow water.

Food: The food of the mooneye consists largely of insects, molluscs, crayfish, small fishes, and plankton.

Comments: The mooneye is not an important game or commercial species. It is caught only occasionally by commercial fishermen and seldom by anglers. The flesh is edible but not valued as food. For further information see Van Oosten, J. Transactions American Fisheries Society, 1961, 90 (2): 170 –174.

THE MOONEYES   family HIODONTIDAE

There are two members of this family in our waters, the mooneye and the goldeye These two species may be distinguished from the whitefishes and ciscoes (which they superficially resemble) by the presence of distinct teeth on the jaws and the absence of the adipose fin. The well-developed teeth will also distinguish them from the alewife and shads. Both species occur only in North America in the waters of the United States and Canada.

GOLDEYE
Hiodon alosoides (Rafinesque)

Other common names: Winnipeg goldeye, laquaiche aux yeux d'or.

Distinguishing features: The goldeye has a deep, laterally compressed body with large silvery scales. The eyes are large and yellow or gold in colour. The mouth is small and supplied with strong, sharp teeth which are also present on the tongue. The sides are silvery in colour, blending to blue or green on the back. The goldeye may be distinguished from the mooneye, which it closely resembles, by the following means: the dorsal fin originates behind the front of the anal fin; the fleshy keel on the belly extends forward beyond the pelvic fins.

Size: The average length of the goldeye is approximately 10 to 12 inches.

Occurrence: The goldeye reaches its greatest abundance in Manitoba and western Ontario. In western Ontario it is found in Lake of the Woods, in the English River, and in Sandy Lake (near the Manitoba border). It occurs also in Lake Abitibi and in the Abitibi River. It has not been reported from north-central Ontario. The first records of goldeyes in the Great Lakes drainage were reported from Lake Temiskaming in 1954. Since 1960 Quebec biologists have reported the species in lakes Matagami and Waswanipi, and others in the Nottaway River system of Quebec. The Nottaway River empties into southern James Bay.

Life history and habits: The goldeye inhabits shallow, turbid lakes and rivers. Spawning takes place in the spring, soon after the ice breaks up. The adult fish move upstream and spawn in the quiet waters of marshy or lake-like expansions. On hatching, the young remain in the quiet water until late summer, at which time they move downstream into larger bodies of water.

Food: Insects (both terrestrial and aquatic) constitute a large proportion of its food, but molluscs (such as snails), crayfish, and fish are also consumed.

Comments: The goldeye is an important commercial species. Its flesh, when smoked, has a delicious flavour and is in great demand. In the unsmoked or fresh condition the flesh is not outstanding and it is seldom marketed in this form. The "smoked goldeyes" (or "Winnipeg goldeyes") offered for sale in eastern Canada are caught commercially in Manitoba or in the Sandy Lake region of Ontario. It is also caught by anglers using a baited hook, small spinner, or a fly. For further information on the early life history see Battle, H. I. and W. M. Sprules. Jour. Fisheries Research Board of Canada, 1960, 17 (2): 245–266.

CENTRAL MUDMINNOW
Umbra limi (Kirtland)

Other common names: Mudminnow, mud fish, umbre de vase.

Distinguishing features: The central mudminnow is a small, robust fish with a sma mouth and soft-rayed fins. The dorsal fin is set well back toward the tail. The body brown or olive-brown in colour (occasionally dark brown), with 13 or 14 irregul black vertical bars on the sides and a black vertical bar at the base of the caudal fi Occasionally, the body is flecked with a blue-green iridescence which is also evide between the rays of the anal fin. The dorsal and caudal fins are dark brown, the low fins pale amber.

Size: This is a small species, seldom exceeding 3½ inches in length in eastern Canad

Occurrence: The species is found in the upper St. Lawrence River and southe Quebec. In Ontario it occurs throughout the Great Lakes, northward to a few miles nor of Lake Nipissing, and westward to Manitoba.

Life history and habits: The central mudminnow is a spring spawning species. Th eggs are deposited singly on aquatic vegetation. The name—mudminnow—is derive from its preference for muddy or mucky bottoms, in which it seeks shelter when alarme It is an inhabitant of the sluggish waters of marshes, pools, and streams and can li under very adverse conditions, such as are found in ditches and isolated pools. I manner of swimming is interesting for it can remain motionless for many minutes, with equal ease it can move slowly in a very precise manner suggestive of a reptile.

Food: It feeds primarily on plankton, aquatic insects, and sometimes smaller fish.

Comments: The central mudminnow is used occasionally as live bait and, becaus of its hardiness, bears up well in minnow pails. It also takes readily to life in a aquarium and will live for many months when given proper attention.

THE MUDMINNOWS
family UMBRIDA

These small, inactive fishes are usually found in sluggish streams or ponds having rich growth of aquatic weeds and a mud bottom. Only three species of the genus *Umb* occur in the world—one in Europe (*Umbra krameri*) and two in North America, *Umb pygmaea* of U.S. Atlantic coastal region and *U. limi* of inland waters. The small siz robust body shape, soft-rayed fins, posterior placement of the dorsal and pelvic fin rounded caudal fin, and cycloid scales are features characteristic of this small famil

CHAIN PICKEREL
Esox niger LeSueur

Other common names: Mud pickerel, eastern pickerel, grass pickerel, grass pike, rochet maillé.

Distinguishing features: Like the grass pickerel, the chain pickerel is very similar the northern pike in body shape and structure. It may be distinguished from the ther members of the pike family by the dark chain-like or lace-like network of arkings on the sides. The back is dark green, shading to green or blue-green on the des and cream or white below. The dark vertical line below the eye is particularly rominent. The cheeks and gill covers are completely scaled.

Size: In the eastern townships of Quebec the chain pickerel may attain a weight f 3 pounds but the average weight is 1 to 2 pounds. The 10-pound, 10-ounce "chain ickerel" captured in McGregor Lake, Quebec, in 1935 and accepted for some time as world record for this species has proven to be a case of mistaken identity. The fish question was a northern pike.

Occurrence: The chain pickerel occurs in Nova Scotia (possibly introduced), New runswick, and southeastern Quebec. Young fish captured in Kingston harbour, Lake ntario, have been identified as chain pickerel but no other record of its occurrence in ntario waters exists. It is unlikely that it occurs in Ontario waters at the present time. also occurs in the eastern and southern United States.

Life history and habits: Chain pickerel frequent quiet, weedy waters of lakes and reams—the same type of habitat preferred by most members of the pike family. pawning occurs in the spring of the year, at which time the eggs are scattered over lant material in marshy areas.

Food: Like other members of the family, the chain pickerel is a predacious fish. It eds principally on other fishes, such as yellow perch and minnows, but will eat variety of creatures such as frogs, ducklings, and mice.

Comments: The species is a desirable game fish in Quebec and in New Brunswick. Quebec, New Brunswick, and the New England states it is commonly called ickerel" and should not be confused with the walleye.

HE PIKES   family ESOCIDAE

The pikes are strictly freshwater fishes that are confined to North America, Europe, d Asia. The five species in the family bear a close resemblance to each other and, in ct, are classified in the same genus, *Esox*. All are predaceous, and with the exception the smaller species (called pickerels) are famous game fishes. Some features charac- ristic of the pikes are: all fins soft-rayed; the posterior placement of the dorsal fin; elvic fins in abdominal position; cycloid scales on body and head; lateral line present sometimes multiple lateral lines evident); jaws elongated and well toothed; gape large.

GRASS PICKEREL
Esox americanus vermiculatus LeSueur

Other common names: Mud pickerel, little pickerel, pickerel, brochet vermiculé.

Distinguishing features: The grass pickerel has the elongate body, long head, an large jaws of the northern pike and, in general appearance, greatly resembles th fish. It may be distinguished from both the northern pike and the muskellunge by th body coloration. The back is olive-green or green, shading to lighter green on th sides. Numerous (10 to 13) dark, wavy, vertical lines or bands are present on the side Below the eye is a conspicuous, black, vertical line. A similar, but less obvious, da line extends horizontally behind and in front of the eye. Both the cheek and the g covers are fully scaled.

Size: The grass pickerel is the smallest member of the pike family. In Ontario, adul average 6½ to 9 inches in length. Lengths in excess of 11 inches have not been reporte

Occurrence: This fish occurs in sluggish streams and weedy bays of the draina systems of the St. Lawrence River (Montreal region and westward), Lake Ontario, Lal Erie, Lake St. Clair, and southern Lake Huron. It has been found in the Ausable Rive Lambton County, Ontario, and in many parts of Leeds County, in the Muskoka regio and in the lake-like ponds on Point Pelee.

Life history and habits: The grass pickerel spawns in the spring of the year in shallo weedy water, soon after the ice cover has melted. Similar to the other members of th pike family, the adults scatter the eggs and then desert them. In summer, it often i habits isolated pools of dried-up streams in the Lake Erie and Lake Ontario regions.

Food: The grass pickerel is carnivorous, feeding mainly on other fishes, particular minnows. Aquatic insects, crayfish, and small frogs are also eaten.

Comments: Because of its small size and limited occurrence, this fish is not we known. When caught, it may be mistaken for a small northern pike.

Another kind of pickerel, the redfin pickerel, *Esox americanus americanus* Gmeli occurs in Quebec in the upper St. Lawrence River. It is similar in appearance to the gra pickerel and may attain lengths of 12 to 15 inches. Until recently, these two fishes we regarded as separate species. *Esox vermiculatus* and *E. americanus*. In Quebec it is als called brochet d'Amérique. For further information see Crossman, E. J., 1962, Roy. On Museum, Contrib. 55, and Crossman, E. J., 1966, Copeia, No. 1.

NORTHERN PIKE
Esox lucius Linnaeus

Other common names: Pike, great northern pike, grass pike, jackpike, jackfish, jack, nake, grand brochet.

Distinguishing features: The body is very elongate and somewhat laterally compressed. The head is large and has a flat dorsal surface. The mouth is large, possessing many long, sharp (backward-pointing) teeth on the flattened "duck-like" jaws. In addition to those on its jaws, the northern pike has patches of teeth on the roof of its mouth. The cheek and the upper half of the gill cover are covered with small scales. On the under side of the lower jaw there are 10 sensory pores or holes. The back is green or dark green in colour, shading to lighter green on the sides and white below. On the sides are many elongate (bean-shaped), light-coloured spots; the young, up to 6 or 7 inches in length, have light vertical bars.

Size: The northern pike averages about 2 to 4 pounds in weight in southern Ontario, but every year fish in excess of 15 and 20 pounds, and over 3 feet long, are reported. The Ontario record pike weighed 42 pounds, 2 ounces, and was caught in Kenora District in 1948. One weighing 42 pounds was caught in Lake Simcoe in 1959 and a 40-pound pike was caught in Nagogami Lake, Algoma, in 1966.

Occurrence: The northern pike is found in New Brunswick, Quebec, and Labrador and throughout Ontario (northwestward to Alaska). It is absent from certain highland areas in Ontario, such as those of Algonquin Park and Haliburton County. (The northern pike occurs throughout the northern hemisphere in North America, northern Europe, and northern Asia.)

Life history and habits: During summer the northern pike is found in the weedy shallows of lakes, frequently hanging motionless just below the surface, but when the waters commence to cool it moves into the deeper waters. Spawning takes place in the early spring, shortly after the ice goes out. Weedy shallow bays and flooded, marshy areas are selected and the eggs are scattered and then deserted by the spawning fish. Female fish live longer and grow to a larger size than male fish—prize-winning northern pike caught by anglers are usually females.

Food: Northern pike feed primarily on other fishes but are not very selective in their feeding habits. Aquatic insects, leeches, crayfish, frogs, snakes, mice, small muskrats, small ducks, and fish of all kinds have been devoured. The fishes most commonly eaten are suckers, yellow perch, and minnows.

Comments: Although alternately cursed and praised by Canadian fishermen, the northern pike is still one of our popular game fishes. In northern inland waters it is an important commercial species. The flesh is white and flaky.

MUSKELLUNGE
Esox masquinongy Mitchill

Other common names: Maskinonge, northern muskullunge, "tiger musky," musky lunge, maskinongé. (The name used in reference to this fish in the statutes of Canada as well as in those of Ontario and Quebec, is maskinonge.)

Distinguishing features: The muskellunge is typically pike-like in appearance, having a long body with a broad back and a long, flattened head, large mouth, and strong jaws. The snout is greatly prolonged and flattened. There are strong, sharp, canine teeth on the jaws and smaller but equally sharp teeth on the tongue and roof of the mouth. This fish may be distinguished from the pike by the following features: the coloration of the muskellunge consists of dark, vertical bars or dark spots on a light background—in contrast to the light spots on a dark background on the northern pike; the cheeks of the muskellunge are usually not scaled on the lower half but are fully scaled on the northern pike; the sensory pores or holes on the underside of the lower jaw are small and 12 to 18 in number (10 on the northern pike). The coloration of the muskellunge varies in different localities. In Ontario the barred pattern is the most common, while in Quebec the spotted effect predominates. the pattern on large fish is often faint. The background colour of the sides is frequently pale green or grey.

Size: Muskellunge over 20 pounds in weight are frequently caught and hardly a year passes that a fish weighing more than 40 pounds is not reported. The average size, however, of muskellunge caught in Ontario varies from 6 to 10 pounds. Mackay (1960) gives 61 pounds, 9 ounces as the Ontario angling record, but the world record would appear to be a 69-pound, 15-ounce fish caught in New York waters of the St. Lawrence River, September 22, 1957.

Occurrence: The muskellunge is native only to the waters of eastern North America. It occurs in Quebec, particularly in the southwestern region; also in the St. Lawrence River westward through the Great Lakes basin to Lake of the Woods. In Ontario it occurs in the following places: Ottawa River, St. Lawrence River, Lakes Ontario, Erie, St. Clair, Huron (Georgian Bay), inland in the Rideau and Kawartha lakes, Lake Simcoe, Lake Nipissing, French River, and Lake Timagami; in the Sudbury District from north of Chapleau to Bolkow on the C.P.R. and in Thunder Bay District from Schreiber to White River and north to the C.N.R. line; in the Rainy River District northward to the English River and in Lake of the Woods. In 1961 a specimen was caught in the St. Lawrence River, off Quebec City.

Life history and habits: The muskellunge lives in bodies of waters of medium size. It is usually absent from the open waters of the Great Lakes and from very small bodies of water, such as are frequently inhabited by northern pike. Spawning occurs in the spring of the year, one or two weeks after the northern pike have spawned. Low-lying, marshy areas, inundated by spring floods, are frequently used as spawning sites. The eggs are deposited in shallow water over vegetation, stumps, and other debris, accompanied by much rapid swimming and rolling by the spawning fish. No nest is constructed and no parental care is given. The eggs hatch in 10 days to 2 weeks, the exact length of time required for hatching depending upon the temperature of the water. When the fish have spawned on spring-flooded land, a rapid recession of the water exposes the eggs and drying will destroy them. During the warm summer weather, the muskellunge moves into deeper water, frequenting the edges of weed beds or rocky shoals. Unlike the northern pike, it frequents the shallow waters in the fall of the year.

Food: The muskellunge is a predatory fish, feeding largely on other fishes and, of course, the larger the muskellunge the larger the fish it will eat. Yellow perch and white suckers form a large part of its diet but many other species of fish are eaten mainly in proportion to their abundance. Pumpkinseeds, rock bass, and even bull heads are occasionally eaten.

Comments: Few Canadian game fishes have the popularity among sports fishermen that is enjoyed by the muskellunge. Its leaping, fighting tactics, general wiliness, size and endurance make it a worthy opponent for the most experienced angler. The experimental rearing of young muskellunge has been attempted but even when small, they are possessed of a voracious appetite. If the food supply is not sufficiently abundant, the young fish become cannibalistic and eat each other. In this respect, they resemble the yellow walleye. The flesh is white, flaky, and flavorous.

The Great Lakes Muskellunge

An Immature or Juvenile Muskellunge

The "True Tiger" Muskellunge

A scientific study of the "tiger musky" of northwestern Ontario strongly suggests that this fish is a hybrid between the muskellunge and the northern pike. The fish has vivid coloration of dark crossbars on the light blue-tinted sides. For further information on the proposed hybrid see: *An Unusual Maskinonge from Little Vermilion Lake, Ontario,* by G. S. Cameron, Contribution no. 31, Royal Ontario Museum of Zoology, 1948. See also Crossman, E. J., 1965, Jour. Fisheries Research Board of Canada, vol. 22, no. 5.

QUILLBACK CARPSUCKER
Carpiodes cyprinus (LeSueur)

Other common names: Quillback, broad mullet, mullet, carp, brême.

Distinguishing features: The quillback carpsucker (a member of the sucker family) has a deep, laterally compressed body, a highly arched back, and a large head. The mouth is small and sucker-like, with thick lips. The caudal peduncle is short, deep, and laterally compressed. The scales are large. The quillback carpsucker derives its name from the high dorsal fin, which has a long base and in which the first few rays are greatly elongated (providing the fin with a pointed or quill-like appearance), while the remaining rays are short. It can easily be distinguished from the carp, which it resembles, by the pointed dorsal fin and the absence of barbels around the mouth. The colour is green or olive-brown above, shading to silvery on the sides and white below.

Size: It attains a weight of at least 3½ pounds in Lake Erie.

Occurrence: The quillback carpsucker occurs in the St. Lawrence and Ottawa rivers, Lake Erie, and Lake of the Woods.

Life history and habits: As in the case of our other species of suckers, the quillback carpsucker spawns in the spring of the year, scattering its eggs freely over a sandy bottom. The adults frequent the shallow waters near the shore where the bottom is silted or sandy.

Food: Its food consists of aquatic insect larvae and plant material, which it obtains from the bottom mud.

Comments: The quillback carpsucker is of only slight commercial importance (classified as "coarse" fish) and of no known importance to Ontario anglers.

THE SUCKERS   family CATOSTOMIDAE

Suckers are found only in the fresh waters of North America and Eastern Asia. They are close relatives of (and probably were derived from) the minnows. Like the minnows, the first four vertebrae are modified, the fins are soft-rayed and the scales cycloid. The mouth is usually inferior, the pharyngeal or "throat teeth" are arranged in a single row (comb-like). Like the minnows, the suckers are forage fishes and provide food for larger predaceous fishes.

LAKE CHUBSUCKER
*Erimyzon sucetta** (Lacépède)

Distinguishing features: The body of the lake chubsucker is laterally compressed. The mouth is small, sucker-like, and directed downwards. Along the midline of the side is a broad, dark brown (or black) band, which is particularly prominent on young fish. This lateral band breaks up into a series of vertical bars or blotches on adult fish. The caudal fins of young lake chubsuckers have a distinct rosy tint.

Size: The average size of adult fish in Canadian waters is not known, but specimens examined are 5 to 6 inches in length.

Occurrence: The lake chubsucker has only recently been found to occur in Canadian waters, although it occurs in many parts of the United States. It has been found only in Lake St. Clair and in ponds and weedy bays (Long Point and Point Pelee) in Lake Erie.

Life history and habits: The chubsucker spawns in the spring of the year in the United States. No details are known of its movements or habits in our waters.

Food: The food consists of aquatic insects and molluscs.

Comments: It is said to be captured occasionally by the commercial fishermen on Lake St. Clair.

SPOTTED SUCKER
Minytrema melanops (Rafinesque)

The spotted sucker was listed by Nash (1908) for Ontario waters, but evidence of its occurrence was not available until Crossman and Ferguson (1963) reported the capture of a 9-inch specimen. It was caught in Lake St. Clair near the mouth of the Thames River in late April 1962 by a commercial fisherman, Mr. G. Archibald. In the United States it occurs southward to Florida and Texas.

Its distinctive colour pattern, consisting of rows of black spots, one per scale, makes it relatively easy to identify. It has a two-chambered air bladder, whereas the redhorse suckers have a three-chambered air bladder.

*The creek chubsucker, *Erimyzon oblongus*, has been often reported to occur in Nova Scotia and New Brunswick. Since recent work has not revealed its presence in eastern Canadian waters, it is considered that the repeated records of its occurrence are in error.

WHITE SUCKER
Catostomus commersoni (Lacépède)

Other common names: Common white sucker, common sucker, black sucker, sucker, catastome noir commun.

Distinguishing features: The white sucker has an elongate and robust body. The sucker-like mouth, which is overhung by the snout and is directed downwards, has thick lips, the upper lip thinner than the lower. The scales are large and generally silvery. During the breeding season the caudal fin and the anal fin of the male have on them many coarse white tubercles (or "pearl organs"). These tubercles sometimes extend to the body and the other fins. The fins are large and dusky. The back is dark (black at times), gold, or brassy, shading to silvery on the sides. Young fish up to 3 inches in length usually have 3 black spots on the sides of the body—one immediately behind the head, one below the dorsal fin, and one at the base of the caudal fin.

Size: The average weight of the white sucker varies from 1 to 2 pounds. Occasional specimens may exceed lengths of 18 inches.

Occurrence: The white sucker is found in Nova Scotia, New Brunswick, and Labrador, westward throughout Quebec and Ontario to the Northwest Territories. In Ontario it is common in almost all lakes and rivers from the Great Lakes to Hudson Bay.

Life history and habits: In the spring white suckers move from the lakes into the streams to deposit their eggs and sperm. Spawning may also take place in the shallow water near the shores of lakes. The spawning fish make no attempt to care for the eggs but release them over stony or gravelly shoals. It is a prolific fish, depositing an average of over 50,000 eggs. The white sucker frequents the shallow (rather than the deep) waters of lakes and spends most of its time near the bottom.

Food: The white sucker eats a variety of bottom-living creatures. The principal food items are aquatic insects, snails and other molluscs, worms, and aquatic plant material.

Comments: White suckers are caught by fishermen in the spring of the year during the spawning "run." Square and circular dip nets, 6 to 8 feet in diameter, are fished from bridges and the banks of streams. At this time, especially, the flesh is sweet but very bony. It is an important food of the muskellunge, northern pike, and yellow walleye. Young white suckers are excellent for use as live bait.

LONGNOSE SUCKER
Catostomus catostomus (Forster)

Other common names: Northern sucker, fine-scaled sucker, sturgeon-nosed sucker, red-sided sucker, meunier.

Distinguishing features: The body of the longnose sucker is elongate, round in cross-section, and more robust than that of the white sucker. The snout overhangs the mouth, and is about twice as long from its tip to the upper lip as that of the white sucker. The mouth, which is directed downwards, has large, thick lips with coarse, pebbly, or papilliated surfaces. The scales are small and numerous and the fins are large. The anal and caudal fins have many course, white tubercles ("pearl organs") on them during the breeding season and also in late autumn. As in the case of the white sucker, smaller tubercles appear on the other fins and the body, including the head. The back is brown to olive-brown in colour, shading to silvery or yellow on the sides, and light below. On the side is a broad, rosy band, which is prominent in the spring and summer, especially on the male fish.

Size: The longnose sucker reaches a larger size than the white sucker and may attain weights of over 5 pounds and lengths up to 2 feet.

Occurrence: This sucker is widely distributed in Canada, extending from New Brunswick and Labrador on the east, to the Yukon on the west. It is found in the St. Lawrence River, in many inland lakes of Quebec, and throughout the Great Lakes (rarely Lake Erie). It occurs in many of the deep inland lakes in southern Ontario and in most lakes and large rivers northward to Hudson Bay.

Life history and habits: The longnose sucker spawns about the same time (and often in the same place) as the white sucker. Spawning takes place in May or June over gravelly bottoms of streams, or in the shallow waters of lakes. It frequents cooler and deeper water than does the white sucker. It is considered to compete seriously with the lake whitefish for food, since both feed on the bottom.

Food: Aquatic insects, small, bottom-living crustaceans, and molluscs are the main foods of the longnose sucker.

Comments: This species is often caught in commercial nets set in the Great Lakes and is usually marketed as "mullet." The flesh is sweet but bony.

HOG SUCKER
Hypentelium nigricans (LeSueur)

Distinguishing features: The body of the hog sucker is slender and rounded. The head is large and broad—often wider than the body. The part of the head between the eyes is slightly concave. The mouth is large and sucker-like and has thick lips. The back is olive-brown in colour, shading to light brown or yellow on the sides. The sides are distinctly marked with olive or dark brown blotches and wide oblique bars, which are directed downwards and forwards. The pectoral fins are large and dusky.

Size: Ontario specimens of the hog sucker average 5 to 8 inches in length. In some parts of the United States it is reported to exceed 14 inches in length.

Occurrence: In Canadian waters the hog sucker occurs only in southwestern Ontario. It is found in streams flowing into western Lake Ontario, Lake Erie, Lake St. Clair, and Lake Huron (northward to the Maitland River).

Life history and habits: The hog sucker frequents the clear parts of streams or rivers where the bottom is stony. Spawning occurs in the spring of the year.

Food: The hog sucker seeks its food on the bottom. It is reported to dislodge the stones and feed on small molluscs and aquatic insects found beneath them.

Comments: Because of its restricted distribution it is of no known importance in the economy of our waters.

BIGMOUTH BUFFALO
Ictiobus cyprinellus (Valenciennes)

In 1957 an 18-pound, 2-ounce specimen was caught in Long Point Bay, Lake Erie, by a commercial fisherman, Mr. L. Schram. Although widely distributed in United States waters, self-sustaining populations of this species occurs in Canada only in Manitoba and Saskatchewan. Like the spotted sucker, this species appears to be only a rare visitor to Ontario waters.

NORTHERN REDHORSE
Moxostoma macrolepidotum (LeSueur)

Other common names: Shortheaded redhorse, redfin sucker, mullet, moxostome à cochon.

Distinguishing features: The robust body of the northern redhorse is deeper than it is wide. The mouth is small and sucker-like and directed downwards. The lower lip is thick. The back is green or olive-green in colour, shading to pale green on the sides. The lower fins, especially the caudal fin, are reddish in colour.

Size: The northern redhorse may exceed a length of 20 inches, but the average is 12 to 15 inches.

Occurrence: The northern redhorse occurs in Quebec in the upper St. Lawrence River and Lake Champlain. In Ontario it is found in many inland lakes and in all of the Great Lakes, and especially in the shallow bays and tributary streams of Lake Ontario and Lake Erie. This redhorse is the one most frequently encountered in Ontario.

Life history and habits: Spawning occurs in the spring of the year, on clean, gravelly bottoms of lakes or streams.

Food: The northern redhorse eats mainly aquatic insects and molluscs which it obtains from the bottom of the lake or stream.

Comments: The northern redhorse is occasionally taken by commercial fishermen, who usually classify it as "mullet" or "redfin sucker." The flesh is flaky and sweet-tasting.

REDHORSE SUCKERS
Moxostoma spp.

The redhorse suckers, or mullets are large-sized members of the sucker family. They are characterized by their large scales (usually 40–50 in the lateral line) and their thickset, robust bodies. Although 7 species are reported from Canadian waters, only two species, the silver and the northern redhorse, occur widely in our waters. Although it is easy to distinguish redhorse suckers from other suckers, the various kinds of redhorses are not so easy to distinguish. Most of the species are more common in the waters of the United States. The flesh is highly esteemed and the more common species are of minor commercial importance.

SILVER REDHORSE
Moxostoma anisurum (Rafinesque)

Other common names: Silver mullet, white nose redhorse, moxostome blanc.

Distinguishing features: The body of the silver redhorse is robust and less compressed than that of the northern redhorse. The mouth is sucker-like, its lower lip thin. The back and sides are silvery in colour. The caudal fin is dusky or gray—not reddish as on the northern redhorse.

Size: The average size of the silver redhorse is 12 to 15 inches. It is reported to attain a larger size than the northern redhorse.

Occurrence: This fish occurs in the upper St. Lawrence River (to below Montreal), in Lake Champlain, in the Ottawa River and, in Ontario, throughout the Great Lakes, northward to Lake Nipigon. It has also been reported from Lake of the Woods.

Life history and habits: The silver redhorse is most frequently found in lakes and large rivers. It is said to spawn in streams and rivers in the spring of the year. Young fish caught in Ontario by collectors have usually been taken from swiftly flowing streams. A pair of large adults were observed spawning in the Chippawa River, eastern Lake Superior, on June 9, 1954, at a depth of about 5 feet.

Food: The food consists of aquatic insects and molluscs.

Comments: This fish is of commercial importance in the St. Lawrence River.

GREATER REDHORSE
Moxostoma valenciennesi Jordan

Distinguishing features: The greater redhorse is heavily built and similar in shape to the northern redhorse. The head and mouth are large. At the base of the scales are dark spots or crescents. The lower fins, and particularly the caudal fin, are red in colour. The tip of the dorsal fin is white.

Size: The greater redhorse is the largest of the redhorse suckers. In former years, fish weighing over 10 pounds were caught in Lake Ontario. The average size at present is estimated to be about 2 pounds.

Occurrence: This species occurs in the upper St. Lawrence River (where it is less common than the northern or silver redhorse) and in Lake Champlain. In Ontario it is found only in Lake Ontario, Lake Erie, Lake St. Clair, and their tributary streams.

Life history and habits: The greater redhorse is said to spawn in May or June in the moderately rapid water of streams.

Food: The food consists principally of aquatic insects and molluscs.

Comments: Its French name is moxostome jaune.

COPPER REDHORSE
Moxostoma hubbsi Legendre

This is a rare species in Canada which occurs in Quebec in the upper St. Lawrence River from Lac St. Pierre to the mouth of the Ottawa River. It was described as a species only in 1952 by Vianney Legendre. Called moxostome cuivre in Quebec, its colour is said to be metallic copper-red.

GOLDEN REDHORSE
Moxostoma erythrurum (Rafinesque)

Other common names: Golden mullet.

Description: The robust body is somewhat laterally compressed. The head is large. The lower lip is broad and not broken up by cross furrows; the halves of the lower lip meet at a slight angle. The body colour is pale yellow or gold. The caudal fin is olive green to pale yellow in colour.

Size: The estimated average length for Ontario fish is 13 inches. (This length is based on 7 specimens in the Museum collection.)

Occurrence: In Ontario the golden redhorse has been found in Catfish Creek, Elgin County, and in the Lake St. Clair drainage.

Life history and habits: In our waters the golden redhorse has been taken only in streams or rivers. Spawning is presumed to take place in the spring of the year in the fast, clear water of streams.

Food: The food consists of aquatic insects and molluscs.

Comments: Due to its rare occurrence, the golden redhorse is of little importance in the economy of our waters.

BLACK REDHORSE
Moxostoma duquesnei (LeSueur)

Other common names: Black mullet.

Distinguishing features: The black redhorse is stout-bodied and laterally compressed. The mouth is overhung by the snout and the lips are thick. The back is olive-green or dark green in colour, becoming golden or brassy coloured on the sides and white below. The dorsal and caudal fins are dusky or dark in colour.

Size: The specimens collected in Ontario (3 in all) are about 12 inches long.

Occurrence: It is a rare fish in Canada and has been recorded only from Ontario, where it was captured in Catfish Creek, Elgin County, and also in a tributary of the Grand River, Oxford County, both tributary waters to Lake Erie.

RIVER REDHORSE
Moxostoma carinatum (Cope)

Distinguishing features: The river redhorse is a robust-bodied, laterally compressed sucker with a large head flattened on top, thick lips, and a prominent snout. The tail fin is red, which will distinguish it from the other redhorse suckers, except the northern and greater redhorse.

Size: Specimens up to 8 pounds in weight have been reported.

Occurrence: Its occurrence in Canada is restricted to the upper St. Lawrence River in the region of Lac St. Pierre and Lac St. Louis, Quebec, where it is called moxostome ballot.

L A K E   C H U B
Couesius plumbeus (Agassiz)

Other common names: Northern chub, lake northern chub, méné de lac.

Distinguishing features: The lake chub is a robust-bodied, chubby minnow, with a small head and mouth. The mouth is slightly overhung by the snout. The paired fins, particularly the pectorals, are large, stiff, and conspicuous. The back is black or dark brown, becoming silvery on the sides, which often display specialized, darkened scales. Breeding males have dashes of red on the forepart of the body, particularly at bases of the pectoral fins and sometimes the pelvic fins.

Size: The average size is 3 to 5 inches, but large specimens may attain a length of 6 inches. Specimens to 9 inches long have been reported from Lake Matagami, Quebec.

Occurrence: The lake chub is found in Nova Scotia, New Brunswick, Labrador, Quebec, and Ontario (and westward to British Columbia). It occurs throughout Ontario (except in Lakes Erie and St. Clair) northward to Hudson Bay. It occurs northward in Quebec to Ungava and eastward to many parts of Labrador.

Life history and habits: In the southern parts of Ontario this species is found only in lakes but in the northern parts of its range it is more common in rivers. In the Great Lakes region, spawning occurs in the spring, usually in April, when the mature fish leave the lakes and ascend streams for spawning purposes. It is sometimes caught by sportsmen fishing with dip nets for smelt.

Food: The food consists principally of aquatic insects and plankton.

Comments: This species is sometimes sold by bait dealers for early spring fishing for such fish as lake trout and yellow walleye.

THE MINNOWS
family CYPRINIDAE

Members of this family are found in Europe, Asia, and Africa as well as in North America. Except for the fallfish and the carp (introduced from Europe) the minnows occurring in eastern North America are small in size. They are characterized by certain modifications of the first four vetebrae and by the toothless jaws and soft rayed fins. They possess "throat teeth" or pharyngeal teeth for grinding their food. These pharyngeal teeth bite against a horny pad at the base of the skull.

Economically minnows are quite important, for besides being of direct use as bait by anglers, many species are eaten by game and commercial fishes and hence are "forage" fishes—a most important role. These forage fishes feed mainly on microscopic life or planktonic plants and animals, thus converting it to a form suitable for food for larger fishes. See key, p. 124 for identification of species.

GOLDFISH
Carassius auratus (Linnaeus)

Other common names: Golden carp.

Distinguishing features: The wild goldfish resembles the carp in general shape and appearance but it does not possess barbels about the mouth, has a less elongate or more stocky body, and is more varied in body coloration. The scales are large and a strong spine is present in both anal and dorsal fins. The basic body colour varies from olive-green through gold (often with black blotches) to creamy-white.

Size: Sizes up to 2 pounds may be attained in parts of Ontario, notably Lake Erie.

Occurrence: Goldfish have been reported from Lake St. Clair, Detroit River, and various parts of Lake Erie. They may occur in any small, shallow lake in southern Ontario (such as Musselman's Lake) as a result of releasing domestic stock. The establishment of a population in Gillies Lake near Timmins, Ontario, testifies to the hardiness of the species.

Life history and habits: Spawning takes place in the spring in weeded shallows, often where willow roots grow exposed in the water. It is a prolific species, and under suitable conditions, such as warm, shallow, mud-bottomed lakes and ponds, may reproduce rapidly. Goldfish, like the carp, obtain much of their food in or on the bottom ooze.

Food: Aquatic insects, snails, crustaceans, and aquatic vegetation are the principal foods.

Comments: Although generally not considered a commercial species, when of sufficient size they are marketed as carp. The goldfish is not, of course, native to Canada but has been introduced as a result of release of pet stock. Goldfish are native to southern Asian waters and have been domesticated by the Chinese and Japanese peoples for centuries. Released stock becomes "wild" after a few generations and often loses the bright gold colour.

CARP
Cyprinus carpio Linnaeus

Other common names: German carp, European carp, mirror carp, leather carp, carpe.

Distinguishing features: The body is robust and laterally compressed. The mouth is of moderate size, toothless, and has the upper jaw slightly protruding. There are two pairs of barbels about the mouth, the second pair, at the corners of the mouth, being the most conspicuous. The body is covered with large, thick scales. The dorsal fin has a long base. At the front of both the dorsal and anal fin is a strong, stout spine, which is serrated on the trailing edge. The colour of the adult fish is usually olive-green on the back, becoming yellowish on the belly. The lower half of the caudal fin and the anal fin often have a reddish hue, with stronger coloration on large adults. Occasionally the scales are enlarged and scattered, or entirely absent from the body, giving rise to the names mirror, or leather carp.

Size: One to 3 pounds are average weights but 5- to 10-pound fish are not uncommon. In Lake Erie and Bay of Quinte carp may attain weights of 30 to 40 pounds.

Occurrence: It occurs throughout the Great Lakes from the St. Lawrence River of Quebec to Lake Superior, and in many inland lakes in Ontario, such as Lake Simcoe, Lake Scugog, and many of the Kawartha Lakes. Captures in the lower St. Lawrence River below Quebec City and in Maine indicate that carp will move into brackish water.

Life history and habits: Spawning commences in early June and may extend into July. The breeding fish usually select shallow, weeded areas of protected bays and backwaters. The act of spawning is accompanied by much splashing and the fish may frequently jump out of the water. The adhesive eggs, when fertilized by the male, are deserted. The habit of rooting about in the bottom ooze not only produces "muddy" water but results in the destruction of aquatic vegetation by uprooting.

Food: The principal foods are aquatic insects, snails, crustaceans, aquatic vegetation, and at times domestic waste found on the bottom.

Comments: Athough not generally esteemed as a food fish there is a ready market for fresh (alive or iced) carp. The flesh is sometimes smoked. Approximately 1,000,000 pounds are landed annually in Ontario by commercial fishermen. A native of Asia, the carp reached this continent via Europe and was introduced into Ontario about 1880. The introduction was, initially, heralded as a fine addition to the fauna, but as has so often been the case with introductions, carp have proved to be undesirable and to be generally detrimental to the production of game and commercial species.

PEARL DACE
Semotilus margarita (Cope)

Other common names: Northern pearl dace, northern dace, méné perlé du nord.

Distinguishing features: The pearl dace is a stout-bodied minnow, resembling the creek chub in size and general shape. The mouth is large (but smaller than that of the creek chub) and terminal and the snout is blunt. On the body are many specialized, darkened scales which sometimes give this dace a mottled appearance. During the breeding season the males have a red or rosy tint along the flanks, extending forward to just behind the head.

Size: The average size is 3 to 4 inches but it may attain lengths up to 6 inches.

Occurrence: It occurs from Nova Scotia and New Brunswick westward through Quebec and Ontario to Saskatchewan. In Ontario it occurs northward to the Lake Nipigon and Lake Abitibi regions.

Life history and habits: The pearl dace occurs in the boggy or brown-tinted waters of lakes and sometimes streams. Spawning occurs in the spring or early summer in streams. Although no nest is built, the spawning area is guarded by the male. The pearl dace seldom seem to occur in large numbers except in boggy pools or ponds.

Food: The food consists of aquatic insects, animal plankton, and various aquatic organisms including small fishes.

Comments: In some waters the pearl dace may at times be a forage fish of some importance for such species as lake trout and brook trout.

FALLFISH
Semotilus corporalis (Mitchill)

Other common names: Chub, silver chub, ouitouche.

Distinguishing features: The fallfish is a robust-bodied minnow, more laterally compressed than the closely related creek chub. The mouth is large, toothless, and slightly overhung by the snout which on large adults definitely projects. In the groove of the upper jaw, near the corner of the mouth, is a small, flat, triangular barbel, which is easy to observe on specimens over 6 inches long. The pattern on the scales of adult fallfish is quite characteristic and consists of a series of dark, crescent-shaped or triangular black bars at the base of each scale along the sides. The colour is olive-brown to black on the back, becoming silvery on the sides and white on the underparts.

Size: The fallfish is the largest native member of the minnow family in eastern North America. The average length of adults is about 5 to 8 inches but large adults may reach 16 to 18 inches in length.

Occurrence: It occurs in New Brunswick and in the St. Lawrence River drainage of Quebec. In Ontario it is common in the eastern Lake Ontario and upper St. Lawrence drainage, and in the Ottawa Valley extending into Algonquin Park. In northern Ontario it occurs sparingly in parts of the James Bay watershed.

Life history and habits: As the name suggests, the fallfish frequents eddies at the foot of falls and rapids, but it also occurs in lakes. Spawning takes place in the spring. The male excavates a nest, the eggs are deposited by the female, and the male then fertilizes the eggs and covers the nest and eggs with stones. At times these stone-pile type of nests may be several feet in diameter and 2 or 3 feet high.

Food: Aquatic insects, plankton, and other fishes are the principal food items.

Comments: The fallfish is often caught by sportsmen when fishing for brook trout, for it will readily strike at trout lures. The flesh is firm, white, and sweet-tasting.

CREEK CHUB
Semotilus atromaculatus (Mitchill)

Other common names: Chub, common chub, horned dace, mulet du nord.

Distinguishing features: The body is round and robust and not strongly laterally compressed. At spawning time the males have up to 6 or 8 thorn-like breeding tubercles on the head and snout. The mouth is large and terminal and extends almost to the eye. The scales are large, and are not shed readily. There is a distinct black spot at the interior base of the dorsal fin. The back is olive-brown in colour, becoming silvery-gray on the sides and white below, often with a violet or purple iridescence on the sides.

Size: The creek chub is one of the largest of our native minnows and adults may attain lengths of 10 to 12 inches, although the average size is smaller.

Occurrence: It occurs in Nova Scotia, New Brunswick, and Quebec and through Ontario into Manitoba. In Ontario it occurs northward to the Sudbury District.

Life history and habits: The creek chub is usually found in clear streams rather than in lakes. Spawning takes place in the spring (when water temperatures reach 60–70°F). The male builds a mound-type nest of stones and, after the eggs are deposited, guards the nest.

Food: The creek chub eats a variety of food, including insects, crustaceans, molluscs, and fishes, as well as aquatic vegetation.

Comments: An excellent bait minnow, this species is hardy and holds up well on the hook and in the minnow pail. It is not of great value as a forage fish since it lives in the warmer trout streams, where its value as food for trout is offset by the fact that it competes with the brook trout for food and even preys on the young to some extent. The flesh is white and of good flavour.

REDBELLY DACE
Chrosomus eos Cope

Distinguishing features: This is a small, round-bodied minnow. The mouth is small and terminal. The scales are small and hardly discernible with the naked eye. Along the sides of the body are two distinct, black, lateral bands, the upper band often being interrupted. The body colours are brilliant—the back is olive to dark brown on top while the lower flanks and belly vary in colour from silvery, or white, through yellow to brilliant red, depending on sex and the proximity of spawning time.

Size: This is a small minnow, averaging about 2 inches in length and attaining a maximum size of about 3 inches.

Occurrence: It occurs from Nova Scotia and New Brunswick, westward through Quebec and Ontario to British Columbia. In Ontario, it occurs northward to James Bay.

Life history and habits: This dace prefers the acid waters of bog lakes, streams, and beaver ponds and is usually most numerous in such locations. Spawning takes place among filamentous aquatic plants and it is thought to spawn twice during the summer season. The eggs are not adhesive and are simply scattered among the vegetation by the spawning fish and abandoned.

Food: The food of the redbelly dace consists mainly of plant material (algae) and, to a limited extent, insects and animal plankton.

Remarks: The redbelly dace provides excellent natural food for brook trout and since it feeds mainly on plant material, it does not compete with the trout for food. It withstands crowded conditions well and, although of small size, it is an excellent bait minnow. It can be propagated in ponds in large numbers. This species may hybridize with the finescale dace. The resulting offspring are usually difficult to identify and grow larger than either parent. Its French name is goujon à ventre rouge.

FINESCALE DACE
Chrosomus neogaeus (Cope)

The finescale dace is a robust, thick-bodied minnow with a large, squarish head and a large mouth. The back is dark brown to almost black in colour becoming silvery to white below. There is a small black caudal spot. Breeding males usually have a brilliant lemon yellow colour on the sides of the body, head, and lower fins. The finescale dace grows to a length of about 3 inches. It occurs in bog lakes, streams, and lakes of New Brunswick, Quebec and Ontario, northward in Ontario to Hudson Bay. This species is usually found associated with redbelly dace and pearl dace. Its French name is goujon à fines écailles.

GOLDEN SHINER
Notemigonus crysoleucas (Mitchill)

Other common names: Butterfish, bream, roach, chatte de l'est.

Distinguishing features: The body of the golden shiner is deep and strongly compressed laterally. The mouth and head are small, the latter being sharply pointed. The scales are large and conspicuous and the lateral line is decurved. Between the pelvic fins and the anal fin is a fleshy keel, over which the scales do not pass. Young golden shiners have a broad black lateral band. On adults the back is dark brown to olive, while the sides have a distinct brassy coloration.

Size: The golden shiner averages 2 to 4 inches in length in Canadian waters but in Lake Erie it may attain lengths up to 6 inches. Southward in the United States it may attain lengths of 10 inches or more.

Occurrence: This species occurs in Nova Scotia (the commonest minnow there), New Brunswick, and Quebec and through Ontario to Manitoba. In Ontario it occurs in all the Great Lakes drainage northward to Lake Abitibi in the James Bay drainage.

Life history and habits: The golden shiner is most commonly found in warm, weedy lakes. Spawning has been observed from June to August and hence the species is considered to have a long spawning period and to spawn more than once during the summer. No nest is built and the adhesive eggs are simply scattered among the aquatic vegetation.

Food: The food consists mainly of animal plankton, aquatic insects, and aquatic vegetation although such items as small snails and even small fishes are consumed occasionally.

Comments: This is one of the most desirable minnows for bait purposes, and is one of the commonest minnows offered for sale in Nova Scotia and New Brunswick. It is also considered to be an ideal forage fish and is used in parts of the United States as food for small and largemouth bass in rearing ponds.

FATHEAD MINNOW
Pimephales promelas Rafinesque

Other common names: Blackhead minnow, méné à grosse tête.

Distinguishing features: This is a small minnow, moderately laterally compressed an having the body heaviest toward the head. The head is large and the mouth very smal and terminal. The scales between the head and the dorsal fin—predorsal scales—ar small. Breeding males in spawning dress have 3 rows of tubercles on the head and gelatinous pad on the head and nape. They may be silvery, brassy, or, in the case c breeding males, almost black in colour. At breeding time, males may have a spot on th dorsal fin.

Size: The average length is about 2 inches but males may grow up to 3 or 3½ inche in length.

Occurrence: The fathead minnow is found from the upper St. Lawrence River drainag and Lake Champlain in Quebec, through Ontario westward at least to Saskatchewar In Ontario it occurs through the Great Lakes basin and Lake of the Woods northward in suitable waters, to Hudson Bay.

Life history and habits: In Canada the fathead minnow occurs most commonly i mud-bottomed ponds and streams. Spawning occurs in June and July, the eggs bein deposited on the underside of boards, rocks, or other underwater objects, and guarde by the male. The females are reported to deposit their eggs in a number of nests rathe than in just one, and the spawning period is prolonged.

Food: Aquatic insects, aquatic vegetation, and animal plankton constitute the mai food items.

Comments: Although sold in many of the northern states as a bait minnow, it i not widely used for bait in Canada. It is readily bred and retained in ponds for feedin pond-reared fishes, such as the smallmouth bass, but it is not of great importance as forage fish because it is not usually abundant in game fish waters.

BLUNTNOSE MINNOW
Pimephales notatus (Rafinesque)

Distinguishing features: The bluntnose minnow is a round-bodied species, being ly slightly compressed. The head is large but the mouth is small and decidedly over-ng by the broadly rounded snout. The scales are large along the flanks but are small d crowded on the back between the dorsal fin and the head. At the base of the l fin a small black spot is usually present. The back is olive-brown to black, becoming very on the sides and white below. Breeding males have coarse tubercles on the snout d top of the head and have a dark, at times almost black, body colour.

Size: The average length is 2 to 3 inches but males may occasionally attain a length 4 inches.

Occurrence: The bluntnose minnow occurs in southern Quebec, through Ontario to uthern Manitoba. In Ontario it occurs throughout the Great Lakes basin northward the Timagami region and westward to Lake of the Woods.

Life history and habits: This species occurs in small creeks, rivers or lakes. Spawning prolonged and may extend from June to August. As in the case of the fathead nnow, the eggs are deposited on the underside of flat stones or boards, on a gravelly ttom in shallow water. The eggs are adhesive and when deposited are guarded by e male. The nests usually contain eggs from more than one female, which probably awn twice during the summer. Each female may lay 500 or more eggs in a spawning riod.

Food: Aquatic insects, animal plankton, and aquatic vegetation are the principal od items.

Comments: This is a valuable forage fish for the game species. Although it is a od bait minnow, it does not carry well and dies quickly in a crowded minnow pail. Quebec it is called ventre-pourri.

COMMON SHINER
Notropis cornutus (Mitchill)

Other common names: Creek shiner, redfin shiner, silver shiner, méné de ruisseau.

Distinguishing features: The body is rather strongly compressed laterally and is dee
The scales on the sides, particularly toward the front of the body, are at least 3 or 4 tim
as high as wide. At spawning time the males have many hard tubercles on the hea
Along the centre of the back is a distinct dark stripe—the mid-dorsal stripe. The bac
is usually olive-green, becoming silvery on the sides and light below. The spawnir
male is brightly coloured with light red to orange on the lower fins and tail and wi
a pink blush on the body.

Size: This is one of the larger minnows and may attain lengths up to 7 or 8 inche
but lengths of 2½ to 4 inches are average for fish offered for sale as bait.

Occurrence: The common shiner occurs in Nova Scotia, New Brunswick, southe
Quebec, and Ontario, westward to Saskatchewan. In Ontario it occurs northward
Lake Abitibi and westward to Lake of the Woods.

Life history and habits: Although predominently a stream species, the common shin
does occur in lakes. Spawning takes place in spring or early summer in shallow, runnir
waters. Often the spawning fish use the excavated nests (gravel depressions) of oth
fish in which to deposit their adhesive eggs. The spawning males are aggressive an
fight much of the time.

Food: Insects (aquatic and terrestrial) and aquatic plant material are the princip
food items, although small fishes may also be consumed.

Comments: The common shiner is very widely used for bait and is a valuab
minnow. It is not generally considered suited to artificial propagation in ponds, primaril
because of the requirement of flowing water for spawning purposes.
One of the subspecies of *N. cornutus* occurring within the area, *N. c. chrysocephalu*
has been shown recently to be a distinct species; see key, p. 126.

EMERALD SHINER
Notropis atherinoides Rafinesque

Other common names: Lake shiner, lake emerald shiner, common emerald shiner, ▪iner, méné émeraude.

Distinguishing features: The body is strongly compressed laterally and moderately ▪eep and the species generally appears fragile. The bodies of fish of 2 to 2½ inches ▪ng are usually transluscent. The head is bluntly pointed. The scales are large and ▪eciduous and come off easily. The anal fin, with 10 or 11 rays, has a long base. A ▪istinct emerald-green coloration, possessing iridescence, covers the back and extends ▪ the sides, blending with a silvery coloration on the sides and white below. The fins ▪e generally clear.

Size: The size attained varies in different lakes but the average length is 2½ to 4½ ▪ches.

Occurrence: It occurs in the upper St. Lawrence River in the vicinity of Montreal, in ▪ake Champlain, Quebec, and westward through all of the Great Lakes to the Sas-▪atchewan River. Northward in Ontario its range extends at least to Lake Attawapiskat, ▪ake Abitibi and the headwaters of the Severn River.

Life history and habits: This fish dwells in large open lakes and rivers but comes into ▪hallow shore waters in the spring to spawn. The emerald shiner often gathers in large ▪umbers in inshore waters and river mouths and around wharves and docks in the fall ▪nd early winter. At times huge swarms of these small fish may be seen side by side in ▪he water to a depth of 18 inches or more but on such occasions the very numbers of the ▪sh prevent the observer seeing the depth to which they occur. During the summer they ▪ove about in schools in the surface layers of the open water.

Food: Plant and animal plankton and insects constitute the principal foods.

Comments: The emerald shiner is undoubtedly one of the most valuable food or ▪orage fishes for the game and commercial species. They are used extensively for ▪ive bait in southern Ontario and in addition are salted and used in the winter ice ▪ishery, for example on Lake Simcoe. Also, it is this species that is preserved (pickled) ▪nd sold in jars for bait. Generally speaking, they are not as hardy a bait minnow as ▪he creek chub or common shiner.

SPOTTAIL SHINER
Notropis hudsonius (Clinton)

Other common names: Spottail minnow, spottail, spawneater, baveux.

Distinguishing features: The spottail shiner is laterally compressed and moderate deep-bodied. The blunt snout overhangs the small mouth. At the base of the caud fin is a distinct black spot which should distinguish it from other silvery, deep-bodi minnows. The black caudal spot is most conspicuous on small and medium-sized spec mens up to 3 inches long. The scales are large and are shed easily. The back is pa green or olive in colour, becoming silvery on the sides and light below.

Size: The spottail shiner is a medium to large minnow. In small inland lakes it m attain a maximum size of 2½ to 3 inches, but in larger lakes, such as the Great Lak it may attain sizes up to 5 inches.

Occurrence: It occurs from Quebec (in the St. Lawrence drainage from about Thr Rivers) through all the Great Lakes, northward in Ontario to Lake Attawapiskat a Sandy Lake (about 53°N. latitude), westward to the Prairie Provinces and the Nort west Territories.

Life history and habits: In Ontario and Quebec, the spottail shiner frequents lak and larger rivers, apparently avoiding small bodies of water. Spawning is said to occ over clean, sandy shoals, or the gravelly sections of river mouths. In May and Jun large numbers may move into stream mouths, particularly at night, and ascend 200 300 yards upstream. It is often the most abundant minnow in northern inland lakes.

Food: Insects, plankton, and aquatic plant material constitute the main food item

Comments: This is a valuable species because it forms a large part of the diet of man of our game fishes; that is, it is an excellent forage fish. It is an ideal bait minno and is the most important bait minnow in many parts of northern Ontario.

GRAVEL CHUB
Hybopsis x-punctata Hubbs and Crowe

The gravel chub attains a length of about 3 inches and is a silvery minnow with haped markings along the side. It is a rare species in Canada and has been recorded ly a few times from the Thames River in Ontario. Although more common in the ited States, it is said to be intolerant of turbid or muddy waters and is less common w than formerly.

SILVER CHUB
Hybopsis storeriana (Kirtland)

The silver chub is a large (lengths to 8 inches), silvery minnow with large scales. At ch corner of the small mouth is a small terminal barbel. The mouth is overhung by ɔ bluntly rounded snout. In Canada the species is restricted to southern Manitoba and ıke Erie waters. It is a forage fish of only minor importance. In Lake Erie it was casionally captured in gill nets but is now rarely seen.

PUGNOSE MINNOW
Opsopoeodus emiliae Hay

This small, silvery minnow has a black lateral band and a black spot on the dorsal se (7–10 rays). It is an exceedingly rare species in Canada for it has been reported ly twice, once in Mitchell's Bay, Lake St. Clair, and once off Fighting Island in ɔ Detroit River. It is reported to grow to lengths of 3½ to 4 inches in the United ates.

SILVERY MINNOW
Hybognathus nuchalis Agassiz

This is a silvery, slender-bodied minnow, growing to a length of about 3 to 3½ inches. ; occurrence in Canada is restricted to the upper St. Lawrence River in the vicinity Montreal, westward into eastern Ontario in the St. Lawrence and Ottawa River ainage, where it seems to prefer wide waters. Spawning takes place in early spring quiet lagoons and backwaters. This species is an important bait minnow in many the northern states and is used to some extent by bait dealers in the Ottawa Valley gion. In Quebec it is called mené argenté. For further information see Raney, E. C., ›39, Amer. Midland Naturalist, vol. 21, no. 3.

BRASSY MINNOW
Hybognathus hankinsoni Hubbs

Like the silvery minnow, this is a slender-bodied species but with gold or brassy flections on the body. It grows to a length of 3 to 3½ inches. It occurs in the upper :. Lawrence River drainage and Lake Champlain westward in Ontario to Lake Erie ɪd northward to Algonquin Park. In Ontario the species shows a preference for ponds ɪd streams with boggy, acid waters. Although a desirable bait minnow in the ırthern United States, it is seldom found in sufficient numbers to be of importance ı Canada. Although in Ontario the species does not occur north or westward of lgonquin Park, its range has been extended in western Canada through Manitoba, ıskatchewan, and Alberta to British Columbia. Its French name is mené laiton. For ırther information see Bailey, R. M., Copeia, 1954(4).

HORNYHEAD CHUB
Hybopsis biguttata (Kirtland)

The hornyhead chub is a thick-bodied minnow with a large mouth, similar to t
creek chub, and with a terminal barbel at each corner of the mouth. The back is oliv
brown to dark brown becoming silvery on the sides. There is a round black spot
the base of the caudal fin. Ontario specimens attain lengths of 6 inches. It occurs
Ontario only in streams of the Lake Erie and southern Lake Huron drainage syste
north to Huron County. This is a more southern species with only a limited occurren
in Canada. In some of the northern parts of the United States it is highly prized as
bait minnow. Formerly called *Nocomis biguttatus*.

RIVER CHUB
Hybopsis micropogon (Cope)

The river chub is a thick-bodied, silvery minnow and is closely related to t
hornyhead chub. Both species are, in turn, similar in appearance to the common cre
chub, but have protruding snouts in contrast to the equal jaws of the creek chub. T
river chub has a terminal barbel at each corner of the mouth. In Canada this speci
occurs only in the drainage systems of Lake Ontario, Lake Erie, Lake St. Clair, an
southern Lake Huron, northward to Bruce County. Formerly called *Nocomis micropogo*

BRIDLED SHINER
Notropis bifrenatus (Cope)

This is a slender, slightly compressed minnow, silvery in colour but with a dark, distinct lateral band. It resembles the blacknose shiner but lacks the crescent-shaped marks along the lateral line. The bridled shiner attains lengths up to 3 inches. It occurs in the upper St. Lawrence River (it is common between Three Rivers and Montreal) and westward in Lake Ontario to the Bay of Quinte. It frequents streams, ponds, and marshy areas. It is a good bait minnow. Its French name is méné d'herbe.

REDFIN SHINER
Notropis umbratilis (Girard)

The redfin shiner is a small minnow, seldom exceeding 2½ inches in Ontario. The body is laterally compressed and only moderately deep. This is a silvery minnow with clear fins but breeding males have a steely blue coloration and the lower fins, particularly the caudal and anal fins, are distinctly red-tinted. There is a black blotch at the front base of the dorsal fin. Although abundant in many of the neighbouring states, in Canada the redfin shiner is confined to a few streams flowing into Lake Erie, Lake St. Clair, and southern Lake Huron. In Ontario it seems to be of no importance as a bait or forage minnow.

SPOTFIN SHINER
Notropis spilopterus (Cope)

This silvery coloured minnow, also called the silver-finned or satin-finned minnow, has a laterally compressed and deep body. The head is almost triangular in outline and the snout is pointed. It may be distinguished by the conspicuous black spot on the membrane of the posterior portion of the dorsal fin. This minnow may grow to a length of 3½ inches. It occurs in the upper St. Lawrence River (Three Rivers, Quebec) and Lake Champlain, westward in the tributaries of the lower Ottawa River, Lake Ontario, Lake Erie, and Lake St. Clair. In Ontario it is more common in rivers than in lakes. Spawning may occur from May to August and the adhesive eggs are deposited on submerged objects. Although a good bait species, it is not sufficiently common anywhere in Ontario to be considered an important bait minnow or forage fish. Its French name is méné bleu.

BLACKNOSE SHINER
Notropis heterolepis Eigenmann and Eigenmann

The blacknose shiner, northern blacknose shiner, or Muskoka minnow is a slender species, growing to a length of only 2 or 3 inches. The body colour is silvery but there is a lateral band which extends along the body, through the eye and around the muzzle. This lateral band consists principally of crescent-shaped bars. The chin or lower jaw is not pigmented. It occurs in Nova Scotia and New Brunswick, through Quebec and Ontario to Saskatchewan; northward to the James and Hudson Bay drainage of north-central Ontario. Spawning probably takes place in the spring and summer. This is a widely occurring minnow in the weeded and sandy shallows of lakes and is probably an important forage fish. It is a bait minnow of some importance in areas where it is abundant. In Quebec it is called méné à nez noir.

BLACKCHIN SHINER
Notropis heterodon (Cope)

This is a slender-bodied, silvery minnow, strikingly similar to the blacknose shiner. The lateral band is in the form of a zigzag line, extending around the head and encroaching on the chin (hence, the common name), distinguishing this species from the blacknose shiner. It grows to a length of 2 to 3 inches. This shiner occurs in the upper St. Lawrence River about Montreal (rare), westward in Ontario through Lake Ontario, Lake Erie and Lake Huron, northward to Sault Ste Marie. Although occasionally sold by bait dealers mixed in with other species, the blackchin shiner is not common enough to be of importance either as a bait minnow or forage fish. In Quebec it is called méné à menton noir.

REDSIDE DACE
Clinostomus elongatus (Kirtland)

The redside dace is strongly laterally compressed but the conspicuous feature is the large mouth, which in proportion to its body size is larger than for any other minnow in the region. There is a broad black lateral band. The red coloration is strongly marked on the sides of males just behind the head, while the sides also exhibit a purple iridescence. It may attain a length of 4 inches. In Ontario it is found only in clear streams flowing into western Lake Ontario. It is of scattered occurrence in the United States.

BLACKNOSE DACE
Rhinichthys atratulus (Hermann)

The blacknose dace is similar in appearance to the longnose dace but the snout onl
slightly overhangs the mouth—i.e., the snout is decidedly shorter than that of th
longnose dace. There is a pair of small terminal barbels. The air bladder is well developed
extending to behind the pelvic fin origin. The back is olive-green to dark brown in
colour and the sides are sprinkled with darkened scales. Breeding males have a rust-red
coloration on the sides. The blacknose dace grows to a length of 3 inches. It occurs in
cool, clear streams of Nova Scotia, New Brunswick, and Quebec, through souther
Ontario to Lake of the Woods. In Ontario it is not recorded north of Sault Ste Marie
In some streams the blacknose dace may be an important food of large brook trout. It
French name is goujon à nez noir.

LONGNOSE DACE
Rhinichthys cataractae (Valenciennes)

The longnose dace is a stout-bodied minnow with an exceptionally long snout and a
decidedly inferior mouth, with thick lips and terminal barbels. The air bladder is not
well developed and extends only to pelvic fin origin. The colour of the back varies from
olive-green to brown in streams (gray in lakes). It may attain lengths up to 5 inches. On
the sides are many specialized darkened scales. It is found in swiftly flowing streams and
occasionally in lakes, from the upper St. Lawrence River of Quebec through the Great
Lakes and northward to Hudson Bay in Ontario and westward to British Columbia. The
longnose dace is often caught in minnow traps set in streams. Although it is used for
live bait it does not live long in a minnow pail. Its French name is goujon à long nez.

ROSYFACE SHINER
Notropis rubellus (Agassiz)

The rosyface shiner is slender-bodied, laterally compressed, silvery minnow, similar n general appearance to the emerald shiner. However, this species has a sharply pointed nout, much more so than the emerald shiner. It may grow to a length of 4 inches. It •ccurs in the rapid waters of streams (rather than the open lakes) from the upper ;t. Lawrence River (Three Rivers), westward through the lower Great Lakes drainage o Lake Nipissing and the North Channel of Lake Huron. The rosyface shiner is not in important minnow in Ontario waters. In Quebec it is called méné à tête rose.

SAND SHINER
Notropis stramineus (Cope)

The sand shiner is a slender minnow, being almost cylindrical in shape rather than aterally compressed, and growing to a length of 2 to 3 inches. It is a silvery form and here is no black pigment about the anus or the base of the anal fin (anal rays—7). In Canada the sand shiner occurs in the upper St. Lawrence River (to Lac St. Pierre), hrough southern Ontario to Lake Nipissing on the north and Lake of the Woods on the vest. This species is found in large rivers and lakes where it frequents sandy shoals. Although of importance in the northern United States as a bait and forage species, it s seldom used for bait in Canada. This species is less common in Ontario than the nimic shiner. Its French name is méné de sable.

PUGNOSE SHINER
Notropis anogenus Forbes

The pugnose shiner is a small (1½ to 2 inches long) but stout-bodied, silvery minnow with a distinct lateral band. It occurs in clear, weedy lake-like ponds on Point Pelee and elsewhere in the Lake Erie drainage and also in the upper St. Lawrence River in eastern Ontario. It is a rare species in Canada and the United States, hence is of no importance as a bait or forage minnow. For a recent review of this species, see Bailey, R. M., Copeia, 1959(2).

MIMIC SHINER
Notropis volucellus (Cope)

The mimic shiner is a slender, round-bodied minnow. It is a silvery fish, having dark pigment about the anus and the base of the anal fin (anal rays—8). It grows to length of 2 to 3 inches. It occurs in the upper St. Lawrence River, through the Great Lakes to Lake of the Woods, and northward to north-central Ontario (at least to Attawapiskat and Sandy lakes). When in abundance, it may become an important forage fish but does not attain abundance or importance comparable to that of the emerald or spottail shiners. The French name is méné à longues nageoires.

CUTLIPS
Exoglossum maxillingua (LeSueur)

The cutlips, or eye-picker, is a stout-bodied, silvery minnow. It may be readily distinguished by the peculiarly shaped lower jaw, which is a three-lobed structure quite unlike the lower jaw of other fishes in the area. It occurs in the upper St. Lawrence River drainage (in the vicinity of Montreal) and in Ontario in the St. Lawrence drainage in the vicinity of Ivy Lea, Leeds County. In this region it occurs most often in fast-flowing streams. The French name is bec-de-lièvre. The name, "eye picker," arises from the belief of fishermen that this fish will pick out the eyes of other minnows held in the same bait pail.

YELLOW BULLHEAD
Ictalurus natalis (LeSueur)

Other common names: Bullhead.

Distinguishing features: The body of the yellow bullhead is short and thickset. The body is more robust than that of the more common brown bullhead. The barbels or "whiskers" on the chin are white rather than black or gray as in the other native bullheads. The caudal fin is slightly rounded. The back and sides are brown in colour, without dark patches or mottles. The lower part of the sides and the belly are bright yellow.

Size: The yellow bullhead attains an average size of approximately ½ to 1 pound in Ontario.

Occurrence: It occurs in the upper St. Lawrence River and in Lake Ontario, Lake Erie, Lake Simcoe, and southern Lake Huron. The yellow bullhead is not uncommon in some of the Rideau Lakes, such as Lake Opinicon, Gananoque Lake, and Lower Beverley Lake in Leeds County.

Life history and habits: The yellow bullhead spawns in the late spring. A shallow, saucer-shaped nest is constructed in the mud, usually located beside or beneath a bank, log, or tree roots. After the eggs are laid by the female, the nest is guarded by the male. Attentive parental care is given by the male until the young are at least 1½ inches long.

Food: Aquatic insects, molluscs, crayfish, and an occasional fish are eaten by the yellow bullhead.

Comments: When caught by anglers it is not usually distinguished from the brown bullhead. The flesh is white and firm and is said to have a delicious flavour.

THE CATFISHES   family ICTALURIDAE

The North American catfishes are characterized by the 8 barbels or "whiskers" (one near each nostril and at each corner of the mouth, and 4 beneath the chin), the strong, sharp spines (one at the front of the dorsal and each pectoral fin), the presence of an adipose fin, and the smooth, tough skin instead of scales. Most of our catfishes are nocturnal in habits and are most active during the hours of darkness. United States waters contain more species and greater abundance of catfishes than Canadian waters.

BROWN BULLHEAD
Ictalurus nebulosus (LeSueur)

Other common names: Bullhead, common bullhead, catfish, mud cat, mud pout, horned pout, barbotte brune.

Distinguishing features: The caudal fin is square. Very strong spines are located on the pectoral and dorsal fins, these spines being saw-toothed on the trailing edges. The anal fin has a long base and is without spines. The colour of the back shades from olive-green to dark brown (almost black). The sides are mottled with darker patches. The underparts are white to cream in colour.

Size: Although well known to all fishermen, accurate figures on length and weight of Ontario specimens are seldom retained. An average weight would be approximately ¾ to one pound.

Occurrence: The brown bullhead is widely distributed, occurring from Nova Scotia and New Brunswick on the east to Manitoba on the west. In Ontario it is found northward to a line between Sault Ste Marie, Lake Nipissing, and Mattawa. The regions of greatest abundance, however, are the warm lakes and ponds of southern Ontario. It is now known to be abundant in Sable or Carp River, 50 miles north of Sault Ste Marie, Ontario.

Life history and habits: The breeding habits of the brown bullhead are similar to those of the yellow bullhead. On hatching, the young (jet black in colour) form a school which is guarded by the male for some weeks. It is a fish of quiet, weedy, mud-bottomed lakes and ponds and slowly flowing rivers where it can tolerate adverse conditions, such as high temperatures and low oxygen conditions, better than most native fishes.

Food: The brown bullhead is an omnivorous feeder. Aquatic insect larvae are taken in quantity during early summer, while crayfish, molluscs, snails, an occasional fish, and plant material form a large part of the diet throughout the year.

Comments: This is the most common member of the catfish family. The flesh is of excellent flavour and is highly prized by many rod and line fishermen. It is taken in commercial quantities in the lower Great Lakes.

CHANNEL CATFISH
Ictalurus punctatus (Rafinesque)

Other common names: Channel cat, Great Lakes channel catfish, lake catfish, catfish, barbue.

Distinguishing features: The channel catfish is easily distinguished from our other species of catfish by its forked tail—all of the other species have square or rounded tail fins. The colour varies greatly according to the environment. Great Lakes forms are light in colour, with scattered dark spots on the sides. The spots are absent on young fish under 3 to 4 inches in length and also on large adults. In inland lakes and rivers, the channel catfish is dark green, brown, or black, shading to light silvery-grey on the belly. The caudal and anal fins of young animals, at least up to 12 inches in length, have a narrow black border.

Size: It is the largest of our catfishes and may attain a weight of 30 pounds or more. The world record is 58 pounds, caught in South Carolina. One specimen reported from Georgian Bay, Lake Huron, weighed 37 pounds. While fish of 10 pounds are not uncommon, sizes of 2 to 4 pounds are average in inland waters.

Occurrence: The channel catfish occurs throughout southern Quebec and the St. Lawrence River, in the Ottawa River, in the Great Lakes, northward in eastern Ontario to the Sudbury District and westward to the Prairie Provinces. In Ontario it is found in larger inland lakes and rivers, such as the French River and Lake Simcoe and its drainage system, to Georgian Bay, reaching its greatest abundance in Lakes Erie and St. Clair. It has recently been captured about 45 miles down river from Quebec City in the St. Lawrence River.

Life history and habits: The channel catfish is found in cooler, clearer waters than most of our catfishes. Spawning takes place in the spring of the year, the adults often ascending rivers for this purpose.

Food: It has a varied diet, consuming aquatic vegetation, insects, crayfish, molluscs, and fish. Such fishes as minnows and yellow perch form a large part of its diet, especially in the case of the adults.

Comments: This species is caught in commercial quantities, particularly in Lakes Erie and St. Clair, and provides sport for many anglers. The white, flaky flesh is highly regarded by many fishermen.

STONE CAT
Noturus flavus Rafinesque

Other common names: White cat, doogler, catfish, barbotte des rapides.

Distinguishing features: The caudal fin is slightly rounded and the fleshy adipose fin is attached for its entire length to the back, in contrast to the free posterior half of the adipose fin on the bullheads and channel catfish. The lips are thick and the upper jaw protrudes or overhangs the lower jaw. The body is covered with a thick skin, which often has a heavy coating of mucus. The colouring is light brown to yellow on the back, blending to light yellow or cream on the sides and white below. The barbels, or "whiskers" are creamy white. It is the lightest coloured of any of our catfishes with the exception of the young of the channel cat, from which it is easily distinguished by the absence of a fork in the caudal fin.

Size: It attains a maximum size of 11 to 12 inches in Lake Erie waters in Ontario. The average size is about 6 to 8 inches.

Occurrence: The stone cat is found in southern Quebec, in the upper St. Lawrence River, and in the tributaries of Lake Ontario, Lake Erie, and southern Lake Huron. It is not a common species, except in the more southern waters. It has also been reported from southern Alberta.

Life history and habits: Spawning takes place in late June. Female stone cats caught in Lake Erie in mid-June contained large and presumably ripe eggs. The nesting site is reported to be located under boards or logs and to be attended by the adults. Although the stone cat is generally found in streams, preferring fast water and riffles, it is also common on mud and sand-bottomed areas in stream mouths and in weedy shore waters (Lake Erie).

Food: The principal food items are aquatic insects, molluscs, and plant material.

Comments: The pectoral spine, at all times sharp and dangerous in catfishes, is particularly so in the case of the stone cat for there is a poison gland located at its base which can cause a painful wound. It is of no importance as a game or commercial species and is seldom caught by anglers.

TADPOLE MADTOM
Noturus gyrinus (Mitchill)

Distinguishing features: This small, stout catfish is uniformly brown to dark brown in colour on the back, shading to gray or brown on the sides and white below. There is a fine black line present along the sides of the body with branching lines marking the outline of the muscle segments. The upper and lower jaws are of equal length. The fleshy adipose fin is attached to the back for its entire length, with no free posterior portion as on the bullheads. The spines on the leading edges of the dorsal and pectoral fins are slender, sharply pointed, and smooth on the trailing edge. The pectoral spine, which has a poison gland located at its base, may inflict a painful wound.

Size: The tadpole madtom is small, averaging only 2 to 3 inches in length in Ontario waters.

Occurrence: It is found in the upper St. Lawrence River (Lac St. Pierre), Richelieu River, Lake Ontario, Lake Erie, and their tributary streams, and in the Rainy River District, Ontario. It occurs westward in Canada through Manitoba and Saskatchewan to Alberta.

Life history and habits: The tadpole madtom frequents mud-bottomed weedy waters of lakes and streams, where it seems to prefer still, turbid waters. Spawning occurs in the spring or early summer.

Food: The tadpole madtom feeds principally on aquatic insects and plant material, found in the bottom silt or mud.

Comments: This small catfish may be mistaken by fishermen for the young of the larger bullheads. It may be easily kept in an aquarium, to which it is well suited because of its small size and preference for still water. In the 1954 edition this species was called *Schilbeodes mollis*. In Quebec its common name is chat-fou.

BRINDLED MADTOM°
Noturus miurus Jordan

Distinguishing features: Although similar in shape to the tadpole madtom, the brindled madtom is more slender. It is gray to light brown in colour with distinct dark spots and blotches. As in the case of the tadpole madtom, the pectoral spines are slender and sharp-pointed and equipped with poison glands at their bases. The adipose fin is attached, throughout its length, to the back.

°*Noturus stigmosus*, a third species of madtom found in the United States, has been reported from the Detroit River, but has not as yet been recorded from Ontario waters.

Size: In the northern United States this species attains lengths of 4 to 5 inches Specimens captured in Ontario have been young individuals of 2 inches in length.

Occurrence: The brindled madtom is a rare species in Canada, having been reported only from the Sydenham River and two streams flowing into central Lake Erie in Ontario. It is a more common species in many parts of the United States.

Comments: The specimens caught in Ontario were taken in clear, fast-flowing waters with a clean gravelly bottom.

BLACK BULLHEAD
Ictalurus melas (Rafinesque)

Other common names: Bullhead.

Distinguishing features: The black bullhead is very similar to the more common brown bullhead, but the body is shorter and more robust. It may be distinguished from the brown bullhead by the presence of a whitish bar at the base of the caudal fin; in addition the pectoral spines are smooth, lacking the saw-toothed projections on the trailing edge. The body is usually dark brown to black on the back, becoming white or yellowish below and never with the blotchy pattern so characteristic of the brown bullhead.

Size: In Ontario waters it attains a smaller size than the brown bullhead, averaging less than 8 inches in length.

Occurrence: Although it is found in many parts of the northern United States the black bullhead is a rare species in Canada and has been reported only in the Lake Erie–Detroit River drainage of Ontario and in a few southern Manitoba lakes. It has not yet been reported from eastern Ontario, although it occurs in Lake Ontario and St. Lawrence tributaries of New York State.

Life history and habits: Like the brown bullhead, the black bullhead frequents mud-bottomed lakes and rivers. Its spawning habits are similar to those of the brown bullhead.

Food: It eats a variety of food, including crayfish, molluscs, aquatic insects, and fish.

Comments: Because of its limited occurrence in Canadian waters, it is unknown to most Canadian fishermen. Elsewhere within its range, the black bullhead is sought by anglers and its flesh is said to have a delicious flavour.

FRESHWATER EELS   family ANGUILLIDAE

The freshwater eel family is only one of about 20 families of true eels occurring in the world, and all but this one are marine. There are about 15 species of freshwater eels, all of which spawn in the sea but live out the major part of their lives in fresh water. Two species occur in the North Atlantic—one in North American waters and one in European waters (*Anguilla anguilla*). About a dozen other species occur in waters of the Indo-Pacific region. The major structural features are: characteristic elongate body shape; soft-rayed fins; the absence of pelvic fins; long dorsal and long anal fins continuous with the caudal fin; and true jaws equipped with small sharp teeth. While most eels are scaleless, the freshwater eels have peculiar cycloid scales, ovoid in shape and embedded in the skin.

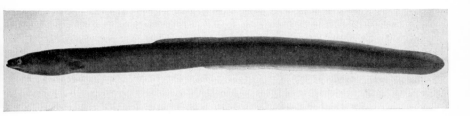

AMERICAN EEL
Anguilla rostrata (LeSueur)

Other common names: Atlantic eel, eel, common eel, anguille d'Amérique.

Distinguishing features: The long, rounded body of the American eel is well known and hardly requires description. It is sometimes confused with the marine lamprey to which it has no relationship. Unlike the lamprey, the true eel or American eel has strong jaws with many sharp teeth. The head is small and there are gill covers present. It has long dorsal and anal fins and a pair of pectoral fins immediately behind the head. The pelvic fins are absent. The back is usually olive-green or brown, shading to pale green or yellow on the sides and light below.

Size: Lengths to 4 feet have been reported but the average length is approximately 2 to 3 feet.

Occurrence: The American eel is abundant in the fresh and salt waters of the Maritime Provinces and Newfoundland and in the St. Lawrence River drainage of Quebec. It also occurs in the Ottawa River drainage and in Lake Ontario. It is presumed to have gained entrance to Lakes Erie and Huron, where it is rare, by means of the Welland Canal. Inland in Ontario it occurs in many lakes that can be reached by tributaries of the Lake Ontario–St. Lawrence River system.

Life history and habits: Spawning is said to occur in the Atlantic Ocean somewhere off the West Indies. The young eels, which are transparent, leaf-life, and quite unlike the adults in appearance, make their way through the ocean to the east coast of North America, where they transform into the typical round-bodied eel-like form. They ascend fresh water streams and rivers to take up residence in lakes and large rivers. They usually inhabit mud-bottomed lakes and rivers. When they have attained adult size, after many years in fresh water, they return to the tropical Atlantic Ocean to spawn and die.

Food: Its food consists mainly of other fishes, although it consumes a variety of other aquatic creatures.

Comments: The flesh of the American eel is rich in oil and highly esteemed. In Quebec and the Maritime Provinces it is of commercial importance. In Ontario waters it is not sufficiently abundant to be of more than minor commercial importance except in Lake Ontario where the catch has increased from less than 50,000 pounds (1956) to about 250,000 pounds (1964).

THE KILLIFISHES   family CYPRINODONTIDAE

The small fishes that make up this large family occur widely in fresh, brackish, and salt waters in temperate to tropical regions in the world. Although common in southern United States waters, only two species occur in Canada. Most species are adapted to surface feeding and have flattened heads and oblique mouths. Some characteristic structural features are: soft-rayed fins; abdominal pelvics; rounded or square caudal fins; cycloid scales on body and head and lateral line pores confined to head; no lateral line on body.

BANDED KILLIFISH
Fundulus diaphanus (LeSueur)

Other common names: Freshwater killifish, killifish, topminnow, minnow (Maritime Provinces), petit barré.

Distinguishing features: This small fish is adapted to surface feeding. The small mouth-opening is toward the top of the head, which is flattened above. The body is somewhat compressed—more so in the posterior portion. The dorsal fin is far back on the body, over the anal fin. The positions of the dorsal fin and the mouth will distinguish this species from the minnows. The body is olive-green on the back, shading to silvery on the sides. There are 18 to 20 vertical bars on the sides, alternately dark green and silvery in colour. It has 4–6 rakers on the first gill arch, the mummichog 8–12.

Size: The banded killifish is small, averaging 2 to 3 inches in length, in Ontario. Occasionally individuals may attain a length of 3½ inches.

Occurrence: This fish occurs in the Maritime Provinces, the St. Lawrence River, and southern Quebec and Ontario. It has also become established in southwestern Newfoundland. In Ontario it is found in Lake Ontario, Lake Erie, Lake St. Clair, Lake Huron and northward to the Spanish River, Sudbury District.

Life history and habits: The banded killifish inhabits the shallow, weedy waters in the bays of lakes and similar locations in rivers. It is frequently found swimming near the surface. At times they are quite abundant in the waters of the eastern counties of Ontario, travelling in schools close to the surface. Spawning takes place in weedy, shallow water in mid-summer. The adults do not protect the eggs or young.

Food: Aquatic insects, plankton (crustaceans), and aquatic vegetation constitute the food of this species.

Comments: The banded killifish is sometimes used as a bait minnow, particularly in Nova Scotia and New Brunswick, and, when abundant, serves as an important food or forage fish for larger carnivorous fishes. As a bait minnow it is hardy and will survive for many hours packed in wet leaves in a container.

MUMMICHOG
Fundulus heteroclitus (Linnaeus)

The mummichog is similar to the banded killifish but is stouter-bodied and has a shorter snout and a rounded caudal fin. Although more often regarded as a salt and brackish water species, it is mentioned because it does move into the fresh waters of coastal streams in the Maritime Provinces, Quebec, and Newfoundland.

ATLANTIC TOMCOD
Microgadus tomcod (Walbaum)

Other common names: Tomcod, Tommy cod, frost fish, poulamon.

Distinguishing features: The Atlantic tomcod is similar to the burbot in general shape, the forward part of the body being rounded while the tail portion is laterally compressed. It may be readily distinguished from the burbot by the presence of 3 dorsal fins (burbot has 2) and by the 2 anal fins (burbot has only one). It may be distinguished from the Atlantic cod by the long filament on the pelvic fin, which constitutes about half the length of the fin, while on the Atlantic cod the filament is less than a quarter the length of the fin. (The Atlantic cod does not occur in fresh water.)

Size: This is a small fish, averaging 8 to 12 inches long and attaining a maximum size of about 14 inches.

Occurrence: The Atlantic tomcod is a coastal species occurring in the salt and brackish water of the Maritime Provinces and in streams and rivers during winter. It occurs upriver in the St. Lawrence to Lac St. Pierre. A "landlocked" population occurs in Lake St. John, Quebec, in Deer Lake, Humber River systems, Newfoundland, and possibly in other lakes of maritime Canada.

Life history and habits: Sea-run fish ascend and spawn in the fresh and brackish water of rivers and their estuaries from November to February, the exact time varying with locality. The eggs, when extruded, sink to the bottom and adhere to bottom materials and to each other.

Food: Atlantic tomcod feed principally on invertebrate animals of many kinds but small fishes are also eaten.

Comments: It is commonly sought by anglers and in winter is the object of a winter ice-fishery on the St. Lawrence, particularly around Three Rivers, Quebec, where 1500 or more huts are set out on the ice.

BURBOT
Lota lota (Linnaeus)

Other common names: American burbot, ling, eelpout, freshwater cod, maria, lawyer, methy, loche, lotte.

Distinguishing features: The burbot is an elongated fish. The front half of the body is more or less rounded but the tail portion is laterally compressed. The mouth is of moderate size, possessing fine teeth. It may be distinguished from all other fresh water fishes in the region (except the tomcod) by the single small, but well-developed, barbel on the chin. The skin is smooth, the scales are small, embedded and scarcely noticeable. There are 2 dorsal fins (the tomcod has 3), the first short and the other long. The body is light brown in colour, becoming dark brown (almost black) in northern and inland waters. Overlaid on the brown coloration are blotches and spots of darker brown or black.

Size: The average weight of the burbot is 1 to 3 pounds. Individuals of 4 to 5 pounds in weight are not uncommon in the Great Lakes but 10-pound fish appear to be rare. A 21-pound, 3-ounce fish reported from Lake of Bays in 1942 may be an Ontario record.

Occurrence: The burbot occurs in New Brunswick, Quebec, Labrador, and Ontario (and northwestward to Alaska). It is found throughout Ontario from the Great Lakes to Hudson Bay. It is common in deep inland lakes and large rivers but predation by sea lampreys has greatly reduced its numbers in the Great Lakes.

Life history and habits: Spawning occurs in January to March in rivers or rocky lake bottoms. Like the lake whitefish and the lake trout, adult burbot seek the deep cool waters of lakes during the warm summer months. At other times of the year they roam throughout the lakes.

Food: The burbot is carnivorous, feeding principally on other fishes. Perch, lake whitefish, ciscoes, minnows, and sculpins form the major portion of its food but aquatic insects, crayfish, and plankton are also eaten.

Comments: The burbot is usually regarded as an undesirable fish, because of its predacious feeding habits and its repugnant appearance. The flesh is white, firm, and delicately flavoured. The fish has a large liver which, when processed, yields a good quality oil, comparable to cod liver oil.

THE CODS   family GADIDAE
The cods are marine fishes that live for the most part in cool seas, except for the species noted here. They are soft-rayed, with two or three dorsal fins, one or two anal fins, cycloid scales, and often with a fine barbel on the chin. Most are predaceous, feeding mainly on other fishes. Many species in the family are important food fishes.

BROOK STICKLEBACK
Culaea inconstans (Kirtland)

Other common names: Five-spined stickleback, épinoche à cinq épines.

Distinguishing features: The body of the brook stickleback is laterally compressed. The caudal peduncle is slender and is also laterally compressed. There are 5 dorsal spines (sometimes 4 or 6), each free rather than connected by a membrane. The caudal fin is round. There is a large, strong spine at the front of each pelvic fin and the anal fin. The body is smooth and without scales. The brook stickleback is olive-green in colour with numerous light spots on the sides. On some individuals these spots are replaced by light, wavy, vertical lines. The body and fins of breeding males may be jet black in colour.

Size: It attains a length of 2½ inches.

Occurrence: The brook stickleback occurs from New Brunswick and Quebec to British Columbia. It is found throughout Ontario, in suitable waters, northward to Hudson Bay.

Life history and habits: This species inhabits only fresh water. It is found in the weedy or grassy portion of streams and pools and is a frequent inhabitant of small bog lakes. Spawning takes place in early summer. Like other members of the stickleback family, the male constructs a nest of small sticks and bits of aquatic vegetation. After one or more females have been induced to deposit eggs in the nest, it is guarded carefully by the small but aggressive male.

Food: The food of this fish consists of small aquatic insects and crustaceans.

Comments: The brook stickleback, although occasionally eaten by other fish, is not a forage fish of great importance. It is an interesting aquarium fish but requires live food. Formerly called *Eucalia inconstans*.

THE STICKLEBACKS   family GASTEROSTEIDAE

The sticklebacks are small, slender fishes which inhabit both the salt and fresh waters of North America although they are primarily marine. They are characterized by the strong dorsal, anal, and pelvic spines. They are of interest chiefly because of their breeding behaviour. As a group they are inclined to be pugnacious.

THREESPINE STICKLEBACK
Gasterosteus aculeatus Linnaeus

Other common names: Twospine stickleback, épinoche à trois épines.

Distinguishing features: The body of the threespine stickleback is laterally compressed and slender. It is variously covered with oblong, vertical plates, which are frequently absent on fresh water specimens. The threespine stickleback may be distinguished from the three other sticklebacks by the 3 dorsal spines (rather than 4, 5, or 9). The first 2 dorsal spines are large, while the third is reduced in size. The pelvic spines are also large. The caudal fin is slightly rounded or square and there is a pronounced keel on the caudal peduncle. This fish is silvery-green in colour and often silvery on the sides. On breeding males the underparts are red.

Size: The threespine stickleback grows to a length of 3 inches.

Occurrence: This species occurs commonly in the salt and fresh waters of the Atlantic coastal region. In eastern Canada it is found inland in the St. Lawrence River and in Lake Ontario, where it inhabits protected bays and river mouths. It does not occur in the Great Lakes above Niagara Falls. Specimens have been caught north of Ottawa in Masham Creek, near Masham Mills, Quebec.

Life history and habits: The threespine stickleback spawns in the spring of the year. The male constructs an elaborate nest of small twigs and other vegetation. When completed, the nest is barrel-shaped, hollow, and with a smooth circular opening in each end. The female is induced to enter the nest and lay her eggs. On completion of spawning, the eggs are guarded by the male, which is said to be particularly aggressive at this time. He continues to guard the young fish until they are able to care for themselves.

Food: The food consists almost entirely of small aquatic insects and crustaceans (plankton).

Comments: The threespine stickleback has little economic importance in fresh waters. In marine waters it is eaten by other fishes, despite its strong spines. It is widely used as a laboratory animal in behavioural studies.

BLACKSPOTTED STICKLEBACK
Gasterosteus wheatlandi Putnam

This stickleback has recently been shown to occur in brackish water situations in many parts of eastern Canada such as Anticosti Island and other localities in the Gulf of St. Lawrence and in southern Newfoundland. Its lemon-yellow colour and black spotting should assist in identification. For further information see Scott and Crossman, 1964. Its French name is épinoche tachetée. (See plate to right.)

FOURSPINE STICKLEBACK
Apeltes quadracus (Mitchill)

Other common names: Stickleback, pinfish, épinoche à quatre épines.

Distinguishing features: The body of the fourspine stickleback is laterally compressed and slender. The body is decidedly deepest in the forward half and this feature, combined with the rapid taper to head and tail, lends an appearance different to that of the other sticklebacks. The spines are characteristically 4 in number (sometimes 5), the first 2 being the longest. Unlike the threespine stickleback, the spines in this species are inclined alternately to the left and right, as in the ninespine stickleback. The back is olive-green in colour with dark mottlings on the sides and silvery on the lower sides and belly.

Size: It attains a length of 2 to 2½ inches.

Occurrence: It occurs in Prince Edward Island, Nova Scotia, New Brunswick, Newfoundland, and Quebec, primarily in salt water but occasionally in brackish and even more rarely in fresh water.

Life history and habits: Although more of a brackish and salt water species, this stickleback does occur in fresh water. Spawning takes place in the spring and early summer when the male is said to build a small, conical nest of bits of aquatic plants and debris. The male is said to guard the eggs and nest.

Food: The food consists mainly of planktonic plants and animals.

Blackspotted stickleback (see account to left)

NINESPINE STICKLEBACK
Pungitius pungitius (Linnaeus)

Other common names: Stickleback, épinoche à neuf épines.

Distinguishing features: The body of the ninespine stickleback is more slender than that of either the brook or the threespine sticklebacks. It may be distinguished from them by the 9 (rarely 8 or 10) spines, which are not in a straight line but alternately inclined to the right and left, like the teeth of a saw. In addition, the caudal peduncle is extremely slender and has a sharp-edged lateral keel on each side. The back is pale green, or gray, in colour. The sides are silvery with irregularly arranged distinct dark bars or blotches.

Size: It attains a length of about 3 inches.

Occurrence: The ninespine stickleback occurs widely in the salt and fresh waters of the northern hemisphere. It occurs from the Maritime Provinces, Labrador, and Newfoundland, throughout Quebec and the Great Lakes in Ontario, northward to Hudson Bay. It is found only in larger lakes in southern Ontario but northward it inhabits relatively small lakes. It is sometimes abundant in the salt water pools along the shores of Hudson Bay.

Life history and habits: Unlike the brook stickleback, this fish moves freely into open water. The male builds a nest and guards the eggs and young.

Food: The food consists of aquatic insects and small crustaceans.

Comments: When in abundance, the ninespine stickleback is of considerable importance for it forms a large part of the food of other fishes. It has been reported that in some lakes it is eaten frequently by yellow walleye and also by brook trout, lake trout, yellow perch, and burbot. For further information see McPhail, J. D., 1963, Jour. Fisheries Research Board of Canada, vol. 20, no. 1.

THE TROUT-PERCHES   family PERCOPSIDAE

There are only two living species of small fishes in this freshwater family. One species, *Columbia transmontanus*, has a restricted distribution in western United States, but the trout-perch is widely distributed from the Northwest Territories southward to Kentucky, Missouri, and Kansas. These peculiar little fishes are called trout-perches because they possess features characteristic of the salmonids and perches. Some structural characteristics are: weak spines in fins; adipose fin present; pelvic fins abdominal and overlapped by pectorals; weakly ctenoid scales and a lateral line present.

TROUT-PERCH
Percopsis omiscomaycus (Walbaum)

Other common names: Silver chub, perche-truite.

Distinguishing features: As its name suggests, the trout-perch has characteristic features of both the trout and the perch families. It is a small "chubby" fish with a large head, mouth somewhat inferior. It has an adipose fin like the members of the whitefish and salmon families, and rough (ctenoid) scales like the perches and sunfishes. It may be distinguished from the latter fishes by the presence of the adipose fin and the absence of sharp spines in the fins; and from the whitefishes and salmon, or trout-like fishes, by the proximity of the pelvic fins to the pectoral fins: the tips of the pectoral fins, unlike those of the whitefishes or trout-like fishes, overlap the bases of the pelvic fins. The body is silvery in colour and somewhat transparent. There is a row of dark spots along the midline of the back, another along the upper portion of the sides, and a third row of more pronounced spots along the midline of the sides. The silvery-coloured lower portion of the sides has a purple or blue iridescence.

Size: This is a small fish, having an average length of 3 to 5 inches in Ontario. It may attain a length of 6 inches.

Occurrence: In Quebec the trout-perch occurs in the St. Lawrence River and its tributary streams, inland lakes, and Lake Champlain. In Ontario it is common in the Great Lakes and larger inland lakes throughout the province, northward to Hudson Bay.

Life history and habits: Essentially a lake fish, inhabiting waters of medium depth, the trout-perch spawns in tributary streams during early spring. In northern Ontario breeding may not occur until July. Trout-perch also spawn in the shallow waters of lakes. In Lake Erie spawning in inshore waters may extend from June to the end of July. In western Canada it inhabits silty streams.

Food: The trout-perch feeds on aquatic insects and small crustaceans (plankton).

Comments: This fish is important food ("forage" fish) for many of the game and commercial species. It is used by anglers for live bait, especially for lake trout in the spring, but unfortunately it does not live long in uniced minnow buckets. Since the trout-perch frequently moves into shallow shore waters at night, it is most easily captured (by seining) at this time. Trout-perch can often be distinguished from other fish remains in predator stomachs because of the unique arrangement of pyloric caeca, positioned in two rows along the gut, 9–12 in total number.

STRIPED BASS
Roccus saxatilis (Walbaum)

Other common names: Striper bass, striper, bar d'Amérique.

Distinguishing features: The body of the striped bass is laterally compressed but not as deep as that of white bass of comparable size. The first (spiny) dorsal fin is distinctly separated from the second (soft) dorsal, with no connecting membrane. The three spines of the anal fin are graduated in size, but the first and longest anal spine is less than half the length of the longest soft ray. There are 7 to 8 distinct horizontal blackish stripes along the sides. The back is olive-green to blue in colour, becoming silvery on the sides and white below.

Size: The striped bass may grow to a large size, and weights of over 100 pounds have been recorded in Atlantic coastal waters of North America. The average size in the St. Lawrence River and Gulf is reported to be 5 to 12 pounds, with fish over 25 pounds being rare. Elsewhere along the east coast 25- to 30-pound fish are apparently less rare.

Occurrence: The striped bass occurs in the coastal waters of the Maritime Provinces, in the Gulf of St. Lawrence, and up the St. Lawrence River to about Sorel. It also occurs in the Annapolis and Shubenacadie rivers, Nova Scotia, and in Grand Lake, New Brunswick.

Life history and habits: This is a coastal species which, in the spring, enters fresh water to spawn. Spawning takes place in rivers, sometimes in a strong current. The semi-buoyant eggs, as many as half a million in a 5-pound female, may be swept along for many miles by the current. Striped bass move about in schools and may travel considerable distances in coastal waters. The striped bass in coastal United States waters move northward in summer (to New England and Canada) and southward in winter. However, most Canadian stocks are thought to winter in the rivers without migrating southward.

Food: The striped bass is carnivorous, feeding largely on other fishes, but various kinds of marine crustaceans are also eaten.

Comments: The striped bass is a well-known and prized game fish to east coast anglers. It is more abundant in United States than Canadian coastal waters. For further information see Leim and Scott (1966).

THE BASSES   family SERRANIDAE

This is mainly, but not entirely, a marine family containing many well-known forms such as the groupers and giant sea basses. They are predaceous fishes of inshore waters in subtropical and tropical seas. Four species occur in North American fresh waters, and three of these range into Canada. Some characteristic structural features are: the two dorsal fins, distinctly separated or weakly joined; anal fin with three spines; thoracic pelvic fins; opercle with a spine; scales ctenoid; lateral line well developed.

WHITE BASS
Roccus chrysops (Rafinesque)

Other common names: Silver bass, bar blanc.

Distinguishing features: The body of the white bass is laterally compressed and deep. The mouth, which is of moderate size, has many small sharp teeth. The lower jaw projects slightly beyond the upper jaw. The first (spiny) dorsal fin is distinctly separated from the second (soft) dorsal fin which will serve to distinguish it from the sunfishes and crappies. In the anal fin, the third spine is equal to, or slightly greater than, the length of the longest soft ray. The eye is tinted with yellow. The back is dark green or gray in colour, shading to silvery on the sides, becoming white below. On the sides are 5 to 7 horizontal dark stripes.

Size: In Ontario this fish averages from ¾ to 1½ pounds in weight. Fish weighing 3 pounds are not common and should be reported.

Occurrence: The white bass occurs in the St. Lawrence River, Lake Ontario, Lake Erie, the Detroit River, Lake Huron, and Lake Nipissing. It has recently been reported from Lake Winnipeg. It is common in many parts of the eastern United States.

Life history and habits: The white bass is essentially a fish of lakes and large rivers. It spawns in the spring in shallow water near shore, or on gravelly shoals. The eggs are not protected by the spawning fish and hatch in a few days. The young fish grow rapidly and in Lake Erie they may attain lengths of 7 to 9 inches in their first year. White bass normally travel in schools, these schools usually being composed of fish of uniform size.

Food: Small fish, especially minnows, seem to be preferred by the adults, but aquatic insects, plankton, and crayfish are also eaten in large numbers.

Comments: The white bass is a game fish of minor importance in Canadian waters only because of its limited occurrence. In the United States it is a popular game fish. When sufficiently abundant, it is an important commercial species in the Canadian waters of Lake Erie. Occasionally, in the spring, it becomes quite abundant in the western portion of Lake Ontario and large numbers can be caught by anglers using spinning gear and streamer flies in river mouths.

WHITE PERCH
Roccus americanus (Gmelin)

Other common names: Silver perch, perch, bass, perche blanche.

Distinguishing features: The body of the white perch is laterally compressed and deep, similar to the white bass. The moderate-sized mouth has many small sharp teeth and the upper and lower jaw are of about equal length. The first (spiny) dorsal fin is joined to the second (soft) dorsal by a thin membrane, unlike that of the white bass. The third (and last) spine in the anal fin is almost as long as the first soft ray of that fin but is only ½ this length on the white bass. The back is olive or dark brown becoming silvery (or silvery green) on the sides: fresh water populations are usually quite dark and less silvery in colour.

Size: The size varies greatly but 8 to 10 inches is estimated to be average, while a maximum size of about 15 inches and 3 pounds is attained.

Occurrence: The white perch was originally restricted to the fresh and salt water of the Atlantic coastal region, and in Canada was found only in the provinces of Prince Edward Island, Nova Scotia, and New Brunswick. However, it has recently been reported in the St. Lawrence River (in the vicinities of Quebec City and of Montreal) and in the United States waters of Lake Erie. It occurs throughout Lake Ontario and also in the lower Niagara River and the Welland Canal. It is the dominant species in the Bay of Quinte.

Life history and habits: Although at home in both fresh and brackish water, the white perch spawns in fresh water in the spring of the year. The adhesive eggs are deposited in the shallows and quickly become attached to aquatic vegetation and other objects with which they come in contact. The white perch is found in brackish water along the Atlantic coast but it is a permanent resident in many fresh water lakes in the Maritime Provinces. Fresh water populations frequently become overcrowded and under such conditions the fish become stunted.

Food: Insects constitute the main food item, but fish (such as yellow perch) are also eaten in quantity.

Comments: It is a popular sport fish in some regions of the Maritime Provinces. The white flesh is sweet tasting. There is a growing sport and commercial fishery in the Bay of Quinte region, hampered only by the apparent tendency of this fish to mature at a small size.

Entrance to Lake Ontario was probably gained about 1950, from the Hudson River (N.Y.) via the Mohawk Valley, Oneida Lake, and the Oswego River in New York State. For a review of the invasion and build-up of this species in Ontario, see Scott, W. B. and W. J. Christie, Jour. Fisheries Research Board of Canada, 1963, vol. 20, no. 5.

SMALLMOUTH BASS
Micropterus dolomieui Lacépède

Other common names: Black bass, smallmouth black bass, smallmouth, achigan à petite bouche.

Distinguishing features: The body is robust, deep, and laterally compressed. The head and mouth are large. There are numerous small teeth on the jaws and roof of the mouth. The mouth extends to below the eye—the posterior end of the maxillary bone never reaches a point behind the eye in contrast to that of the largemouth bass. There are 3 stiff spines on the front of the anal fin. The spines in the spiny portion of the dorsal fin are short and of a more uniform length, and the spiny and soft-rayed portions of the fin are more broadly joined together, than those of the largemouth bass. The markings on the smallmouth bass are also distinctive. On the sides, especially in younger fish, are distinct vertical bars which are sometimes broken to give a spotted effect on the upper portion of the sides. Fingerlings have very distinct vertical bars and a characteristically marked caudal fin, which is orange coloured at the base bordered with black, and clear, or white, toward the tip. The markings, however, may fade one moment and be strikingly evident the next, depending on the mood of the fish. The overall coloration of this fish varies greatly with environment. For example, those from Lake Erie and large weedy lakes are usually pale green, while fish from smaller, peat-stained waters of inland lakes are brown or dark brown in colour.

Size: In Ontario the average weight of smallmouth bass is 1½ to 2½ pounds. Four-pound fish are not uncommon and every few years 7-pound fish are reported. Until recently an 8-pound fish was the largest reported for Ontario but in 1951 a smallmouth bass weighing 9 pounds, 2 ounces, was caught in Macauley Lake, Nipissing District, Ontario. In 1954 a 9-pound, 13½-ounce fish was caught in Birch Lake, Haliburton County, and is believed to be a Canadian record. The world's record smallmouth bass weighed 11 pounds, 15 ounces, and was caught in Kentucky in 1955. The 11-pound, 3-ounce fish caught in 1964 and listed as a smallmouth, was, in fact, a sheepshead.

Occurrence: In Canada the smallmouth bass was originally confined to the St. Lawrence River and Great Lakes drainage system of Quebec and Ontario. The species was found in southern Ontario, northward to slightly beyond Lake Nipissing. A population also existed south of Lake Nipigon. Because of its popularity, it was widely introduced into other waters such as Lake of the Woods, where planting was commenced about 1901. The smallmouth bass is now established in Canada from Nova Scotia westward to at least Saskatchewan and, in Ontario, northward to the Timiskaming District and Lake Nipigon. Within the province of Ontario it is particularly well established in the Thousand Islands district of the St. Lawrence River, around the islands of western Lake Erie, in Georgian Bay, Lake Nipissing, and other inland lakes in southern Ontario.

Life history and habits: The smallmouth bass reaches its greatest abundance in rock lakes and rivers. The most favourable conditions are found in clear, rocky lakes, having depths in excess of 25 or 30 feet, with sparse aquatic vegetation and rocky or gravelly shoals. Lakes which become excessively warm (over 80°F), or remain cool (below 60°F), in summer are not well suited to this species. Weedy, mud-bottomed lakes are generally, not too productive of smallmouth bass because the fish require the rock or gravelly areas on the bottom upon which to construct their nests. The time at which spawning begins is determined largely by the temperature of the water, as is the case with so many fishes. In southern Ontario water temperatures of 60° to 70°F are usually reached during the month of June and spawning then takes place. Spawning may be delayed until late June, and even extend into July, in years when the spring season is unusually cool. The nest is built by the male on a stony or gravelly bottom, swept clean by using the caudal fin to create a strong current of water over the particular site. The current carries away silt, leaves, and debris and, after considerable effort, a shallow depression, lined with clean rock or gravel, is obtained. A mature female is enticed over the nest, the eggs are deposited and fertilized, and the female is driven off. This action may be repeated until the eggs from as many as three females are deposited in the same nest. In the female all of the eggs do not ripen simultaneously, thereby necessitating more than one spawning. When spawning is completed, the male jealously guards the nest and eggs, driving off all intruders. When the eggs hatch he also guards the young, watchfully swimming about the school and keeping eager predators away. The fry remain under the protective care of the male for one or two weeks and are then left to fend for themselves. They are usually about ½ inch long when they are abandoned. The male is particularly susceptible to anglers' bait when guarding the nest and young because, although he may not feed, he will attack anything moving in the vicinity of the nest. If he is removed the eggs or young will be destroyed by predators.

Food: The smallmouth bass is carnivorous. Large adults feed almost entirely on other fishes but medium-sized fish may supplement the fish diet with crayfish. At times, crayfish may constitute more than 50 per cent of the diet, particularly in those waters where crayfish are abundant. Yellow perch, various species of minnows, young sunfish, and sticklebacks are some of the fishes most commonly eaten, but the species of fish and the amount eaten depends upon their abundance and availability. In many waters leeches are also eaten in quantity. Fingerlings normally consume large numbers of aquatic and terrestrial insects.

Comments: The smallmouth bass is the most popular game fish to the average Ontario sportsman because of its superb fighting qualities, its preference for shallow water and its readiness to strike at a bait or lure throughout the summer months.

THE SUNFISHES   family CENTRARCHIDAE

This relatively small family of strictly freshwater fishes is native to the warm lakes and rivers of North America, although some species, particularly the so-called black basses, have been introduced into fresh waters around the world. In North America, some members of the family occur from Lake Abitibi and Lake Winnipeg southward to Florida and the Gulf states. These popular game fishes are largely predaceous. They are of additional interest because they nest in a shallow depression and the male usually maintains a rigid guard over eggs and young. Some structural characteristics of the sunfishes are: dorsal fin of spiny and soft-rayed portions usually joined, sometimes separated by a notch; anal fin rays preceded by 3, 4, 5, or 6 spines; pelvic fins thoracic in position; opercle without a spine; scales ctenoid; lateral line well developed.

LARGEMOUTH BASS
Micropterus salmoides (Lacépède)

Other common names: Green bass, largemouth black bass, largemouth, achigan à ande bouche.

Distinguishing features: The body of the largemouth bass is similar in shape to that of e smallmouth bass but large fish are sometimes deeper-bodied. It may be distinguished om the smallmouth bass by the larger mouth, which extends beyond the eye—the end the maxillary bone reaches a point behind the eye. In addition, the spiny dorsal fin often higher and the spines are not as uniform in length. The spiny portion is almost parated from the soft-rayed portion of the fin by a prominent notch. Instead of the rtical bars of the smallmouth bass, the largemouth bass, especially young fish, have broad dark lateral band. The basic colour is usually dark green on the back, shading lighter green on the sides and light-coloured below. The dark irregular band along the le is evident on small fish but on large adults it may be inconspicuous or absent.

Size: The average size of fish caught in Ontario varies from 2 to 3 pounds, but fish eighing 3 to 4 pounds are not uncommon. Specimens approximately 6 pounds in eight are reported every year, and 7- and 8-pound fish are occasionally caught. The cord for this species is a 22-pound, 4-ounce fish caught in Georgia in 1932. The ntario record is a 14-pound, 2-ounce fish caught in Stoney Lake, Peterborough County, 1948.

Occurrence: The largemouth bass is native to many waters in southern Quebec and ntario. In Ontario it occurs northward to Lake Temiskaming. It is also found in the gion south of Lake Nipigon and in the Lake of the Woods district, where its currence is believed to be due to plantings or introduction. In Ontario it is common the Kawartha and Rideau Lake districts and in many warm, weedy inland lakes.

Life history and habits: This fish prefers warmer, weedier waters than the smallmouth iss and it is also more tolerant of turbid or silted conditions. The spawning habits of the vo species are similar. The largemouth bass chooses a nesting site on a mud or marl ottom and often on water-lily roots exposed by the sweeping action of the male. The gs and young are guarded zealously for a time and then abandoned and the young lowed to fend for themselves.

Food: Fish are most important in the diet of adults but crayfish and frogs are also ten. Insects are eaten in considerable numbers by small fish.

Comments: The largemouth bass is an excellent game fish but individuals taken in uggish waters are generally less active and less spectacular when hooked than small-outh bass of comparable size. It is not as abundant in Ontario as the better-known nallmouth bass.

ROCK BASS
Ambloplites rupestris (Rafinesque)

Other common names: Northern rock bass, redeye, redeye bass, crapet de roche.

Distinguishing features: The rock bass is laterally compressed but not as marked as the sunfishes. The eyes are large and reddish in colour. The body is olive-brown with darker blotches or mottlings, the young especially showing conspicuous dark blotches on the sides. Each of the scales along the sides has a rather large dark spot which fades out towards the belly. There are 6 (occasionally 5 or 7) spines in the anal fin (3 in the sunfishes) and, with the exception of the pectoral and pelvic fins, all fins are dusky and spotted.

Size: Lengths of from 10 to 12 inches and weights of a pound have been recorded but the average length is 6 to 8 inches and the average weight approximately ½ pound.

Occurrence: In Quebec the rock bass occurs in the upper St. Lawrence River drainage and in Lake Champlain. In Ontario it is found in all of the Great Lakes, northward to Lake Abitibi in the east and the English River in the west (occurring in the southern parts of Manitoba to lower Lake Winnipeg westward to southern Saskatchewan). It does not occur in Lake Nipigon. The rock bass is abundant in Lake Ontario and Georgian Bay waters.

Life history and habits: The rock bass is most frequently found in the rocky shallows of lakes. Spawning takes place in spring or early summer, when water temperatures reach 60° to 70°F. The male builds a circular nest on the gravelly bottom in shallow water. The female deposits the eggs, which are guarded by the male; when hatched the young are also guarded for a short time. The adults often move about in schools. The rock bass is commonly found in the same waters with smallmouth bass and, to a lesser extent, the pumpkinseed.

Food: The food consists largely of aquatic insects, crayfish, and small fish.

Comments: Although not generally considered an important game fish, and caught only incidentally while fishing for other species (especially smallmouth bass), the rock bass provides fair sport and the flesh is white, flaky, and of good flavour.

BLUEGILL
Lepomis macrochirus Rafinesque

Other common names: Bluegill sunfish, blue sunfish, sunfish, bream,* roach,* crapet oreilles bleues.

Distinguishing features: The body is deep and laterally compressed. The mouth is small, barely reaching a point in line with the front of the eye. The opercular flap is short and dark in colour, sometimes with a purple hue but lacking a scarlet spot or margin. On the membrane between the last few rays of the soft dorsal fin are a series of oblong blotches, which may merge or blend together to form a single large blotch. There are 3 spines preceding the soft rays in the anal fin. The back is blue-green to olive-green in colour, becoming lighter on the sides, and often becoming orange to yellow on the "throat" or "breast." A series of vertical bars may be evident on the sides.

Size: The bluegill is the largest of our sunfishes and is reported to attain lengths of 10 or 12 inches, especially in the Rideau district.

Occurrence: In Quebec it is found in the Lake Champlain and upper St. Lawrence drainages. In Ontario it occurs in the St. Lawrence River, Lake Ontario, Lake Erie, and Lake St. Clair drainage systems. It is abundant and of large size in many of the Rideau lakes. In 1956 specimens were caught in Quetico Provincial Park, Rainy River District, Ontario.

Life history and habits: The bluegill inhabits the warm weedy waters of protected bays, ponds, and lakes. Like its close relatives, this species spawns in the spring, the male constructing a nest on gravelly bottoms in shallow water. The female deposits the eggs in the nest but it is the male that carefully guards the eggs and the young fish.

Food: Aquatic insects and small crayfish are the principal food items.

Comments: The bluegill is not well known to most Canadian fishermen, although it is a popular pan fish in many parts of the northern United States. While it cannot compete in size with the largemouth and smallmouth bass it is a strong fighter and the flesh is of good quality.

---

*The names, bream and roach, properly belong to species of minnows found in England and other parts of Europe.

PUMPKINSEED
Lepomis gibbosus (Linnaeus)

Other common names: Common sunfish, yellow sunfish, sunfish, crapet-soleil.

Distinguishing features: The body is laterally compressed and is more round in out line than any of our other sunfishes. The mouth is small, extending back only to th anterior margin of the eye. The teeth are small. The cheeks and opercles have streak or lines of brilliant blue which are especially prominent on the males. The opercula flap is dark in colour with a brilliant scarlet spot on the posterior margin. The body i sprinkled with rust-coloured scales. Several vertical bars frequently occur on the side of the young fish and are often visible on mature females. The pectoral fins are clea and the tips are pointed. The remaining fins are dusky, often with brown spots, especiall on the dorsal.

Size: The pumpkinseed inhabitating lakes may reach a length of 8 to 9 inches but i streams and small ponds, where they frequently become overpopulated, adults reac only 4 or 5 inches in length.

Occurrence: The pumpkinseed is the most common and most widely distributed o our sunfishes. It occurs in New Brunswick, throughout southern Quebec and Ontario northward in Ontario to the Sault Ste Marie and Timagami regions.

Life history and habits: The pumpkinseed is found most frequently in weedy ponds lakes, and slowly flowing rivers. In the spring the male energetically sweeps away th gravel and debris from the bottom, using the caudal fin in the manner of a whisk thus constructing a shallow depression which serves as the nest. The eggs are expelle over the nest by the female, are fertilized, and then guarded by the male. When th eggs hatch, the young are also guarded for a short time. Like all of the sunfishes, th male is very aggressive at spawning time.

Food: The food consists mainly of aquatic insects, snails and other invertebrat animals, and, occasionally, small fishes.

Comments: Although not considered to be a game fish, the pumpkinseed has ofter provided the angler with his first thrill of a line slicing through the water. It is occasion ally taken in numbers by commercial seine fishermen, who usually find a ready marke for it. The flesh is sweet and of excellent flavour.

LONGEAR SUNFISH
Lepomis megalotis (Rafinesque)

Other common names: Great Lakes longear sunfish.

Distinguishing features: The body of the longear sunfish is short, deep, and laterally impressed. As its name suggests, this species has a long opercular flap or "ear," though specimens from Canadian waters have a shorter flap than those from many of the bordering states. The flap is dark brown, almost black at times, with a narrow red order. It is a colourful sunfish, with flecks or spots of yellow and blue on the sides id irregular lines of blue or green on the cheeks.

Size: It is a small fish, averaging only 3 to 4 inches long in Canadian waters.

Occurrence: The longear sunfish occurs in parts of the Upper St. Lawrence River Quebec. In Ontario it has been found only in the Lake Erie, Lake St. Clair, and iuthern Georgian Bay regions. It has recently been shown to occur in the Rainy River istrict, Ontario. Although it is nowhere abundant within the area described, it is most equently caught in Lake Erie district.

Life history and habits: The longear sunfish lives in clear, weedy streams, ponds, id bays. Spawning takes place in the spring, at which time the male builds a shallow est in shore waters.

Food: The food of this sunfish in Canadian waters is not known, but in the northern nited States it is reported to feed principally on aquatic insects.

Comments: Like the green sunfish, the longear sunfish is not well known to Canadian shermen due to its restricted occurrence and small size and hence cannot be con- dered a game species of even minor importance. The form occurring in Canadian waters the subspecies, *L. m. peltastes*. For further information see Gruchy, C., and W. B. cott, Jour. Fisheries Research Board of Canada, vol. 23, no. 9, 1966.

GREEN SUNFISH
Lepomis cyanellus Rafinesque

Distinguishing features: The green sunfish has a robust body in comparison with our ommon sunfish, the pumpkinseed. The dorsal fin is composed of spiny and soft rays s in the pumpkinseed, and the soft rays in the anal fin are preceded by 3 spines. The iouth is larger than that of any of our species of sunfishes, extending to a point eneath the middle of the eye. The opercular flap is large, the posterior portion marked y a light-coloured border. The colour of the back is olive-green, shading to lighter reen on the sides. Flecks of iridescent green or blue-green are located on the cheeks nd on a few of the scales on the sides.

Size: Specimens up to 5 inches long have been caught in Ontario.

Occurrence: The green sunfish occurs throughout many of the bordering states of the Jnited States but it is of rare occurrence in Canadian waters. It has been found in the 'hames watershed in the county of Perth, Ontario, where it is restricted to small lakes, otably those at the head of the Avon River, and also some small lakes in Bruce County,)ntario. Specimens caught in 1956 indicate that it occurs in Quetico Provincial Park, tainy River District, Ontario.

Life history and habits: Like its close relatives, the green sunfish spawns in the pring of the year, the male constructing a small, shallow nest on the bottom in inshore /aters.

Food: Its food in Canadian waters is not known but elsewhere it is reported to feed n insects and small fishes.

Comments: This sunfish is not well known to Canadian anglers because of its estricted occurrence.

YELLOWBELLY SUNFISH
Lepomis auritus (Linnaeus)

Distinguishing features: The body of the yellowbelly sunfish is strongly lateral compressed and deep, similar to the common pumpkinseed and other sunfishes. T "ear-flap" is moderately long, blue-black in colour, and has no red coloration on (thus differing from that of the pumpkinseed); the colour of the belly varies fro yellow to brilliant orange-red.

Size: Specimens caught in New Brunswick range from 5 to 7 inches in length. the neighbouring state of Maine, U.S.A., the yellowbelly sunfish is said rarely attain a length over 6 inches.

Occurrence: In Canada this species has been reported only from New Brunswic where it was first collected by Mr. H. White in the Canaan and Kennebecasis rivers the Saint John River system. It is also known to occur in Lake Oromocto, York Count and in Oromocto River and South Oromocto River, Sunbury County. Additional collecti will doubtless extend its known range.

Life history and habits: Although the breeding habits in Canada are not known, the United States the yellowbelly sunfish spawns in the spring of the year at whi time the male constructs a shallow nest, as is the case with other sunfishes. T adhesive eggs are deposited in the nest by the female, and after fertilizing them t male guards the eggs and later, for a short time, the young.

Food: Adult and larval insects, molluscs, and small fishes probably constitute a lar proportion of the diet.

Comments: Due to its very limited occurrence this species is relatively unknown New Brunswick fishermen.

BLACK CRAPPIE
Pomoxis nigromaculatus (LeSueur)

Other common names: Crappie, calico bass, Oswego bass, strawberry bass, speckled bass, shiner, crapet calicot.

Distinguishing features: The black crappie is deep-bodied and laterally compressed. There is a "forehead" depression immediately above the eyes. The spines in the dorsal fin are 7 to 8 in number (compared with 6 in the white crappie). The general coloration is dark green to black on the back, the sides silvery with irregularly arranged dark green or black spots or small blotches. There are dark green speckles on the dorsal, anal, and caudal fins. Except on young of the year, the dark spots or blotches are not arranged in vertical bands, as in the white crappie.

Size: Large black crappies may weigh 2 pounds and reach 12 to 14 inches in length, but the average is closer to ½ pound and 7 to 10 inches in length.

Occurrence: The black crappie occurs more widely in Canadian waters than does the white crappie. It is found in the upper St. Lawrence River, eastward to Lac St. Pierre in Quebec, in the Ottawa River, Lake Ontario, Lake Erie and Lake St. Clair and tributary waters, Lake of the Woods district and into southern Manitoba. It is common in many of the Rideau Lakes in the counties of Frontenac and Leeds, Ontario, where it probably reaches its greatest abundance in Canadian waters. It has recently become established in Black and Nipigon bays, northern Lake Superior.

Life history and habits: The black crappie, which spawns in late spring and early summer, is a nest builder, the nest being constructed in water of from 3 to 6 feet in depth, on sandy or silted bottom, among rooted aquatic plants. It is a fish of the quiet waters of lakes, ponds, and slow-moving streams, usually where there is a good growth of aquatic plants. It is a gregarious species and often travels in schools.

Food: Small fishes and aquatic insects are the principal food items.

Comments: In southern and eastern Ontario it provides excellent sport and it is popular among winter anglers in Lake of the Woods region. Live minnows are used as bait. The flesh is exceedingly sweet and flavorous.

WHITE CRAPPIE
Pomoxis annularis Rafinesque

Other common names: Crappie, silver bass, white bass.

Distinguishing features: The white crappie is similar in appearance to the black crappie but may be distinguished from it by the presence of 6 spines in the dorsal fin (7 or 8 in the black crappie). The body is laterally compressed. It is more elongate than the black crappie or the sunfishes. The mouth is large and bears many fine teeth. The "forehead" is depressed, a feature more readily noted when the fish is viewed from the side. The body colouring is dark green to black on the back, becoming silvery on the sides with dark green or black blotches usually arranged as vertical stripes, which are often inconspicuous on large adults. The dorsal, caudal, and anal fins bear dark spots or mottlings.

Size: Sizes up to 10 to 12 inches in length and almost a pound in weight have been reported but the average size is approximately 7 to 10 inches.

Occurrence: The white crappie is found in the western drainage of Lake Ontario, throughout the Lake Erie drainage, and in Lake St. Clair. The most northern record for Ontario is a specimen recently (1950) received from South Bay on Manitoulin Island. This species is most frequently found in muddy or silted streams and lakes. In Lakes Erie and Ontario it is usually found in stream mouths and weedy, protected bays. It is not abundant in any Ontario waters.

Life history and habits: The white crappie is similar to the black crappie in its habits. It is a nest-building species, spawning in spring and early summer.

Food: Aquatic insects, plankton, and fishes constitute the major portion of its diet. The adults feed heavily on smaller fishes.

Comments: The white crappie is less common than the black crappie and is often mistaken for it. Its flesh is of excellent quality but the species does not occur in sufficient numbers to be considered an important game or commercial fish.

BLUE WALLEYE
Stizostedion vitreum glaucum Hubbs

Other common names: Blue pickerel, blue pike, blue pikeperch, "blue."

Distinguishing features: In general appearance, in so far as fins, scaling, mouth, teeth, and other features are concerned, the blue walleye closely resembles the yellow walleye. The major point of difference is the slate-blue body colour of this species. In addition, the pelvic fins are white in colour in contrast to the cream-coloured pelvic fins of the yellow walleye. Other points of difference, although not useful as distinguishing features, are the slower rate of growth, smaller maximum size, and different spawning time of the blue walleye.

Size: The average size of the blue walleye is approximately ½ to one pound. Records of maximum sizes are not available.

Occurrence: The blue walleye occurs in Lake Erie, where it was formerly abundant, and in Lake Ontario and the Niagara River.

Life history and habits: In Lake Erie spawning usually takes place in shallow water in May. The spawning fish do not prepare a nest, nor do they protect the eggs. The blue walleye grows more slowly and inhabits deeper waters than the yellow walleye. Maturity is attained at a length of 12 to 13 inches.

Food: This species is carnivorous, feeding largely on other fishes. The principal fishes eaten are yellow perch, American smelt, trout-perch, and minnows, particularly the emerald shiner. During the summer months large numbers of mayflies are consumed.

Comments: The blue walleye was a commercial fish of considerable importance in Lake Erie and, to a lesser extent, in Lake Ontario. However, pollution and other environmental changes have succeeded in destroying this species and it is now rare or extinct. Bluish-coloured yellow walleyes occasionally reported from such inland lakes as Nipissing are varieties of the yellow walleye and not identical with the blue walleye, S. v. glaucum. The flesh had an excellent flavour.

THE PERCHES   family PERCIDAE

The perches are found in the freshwater lakes and rivers of North America, Europe, and Asia. The family is often divided into two or three separate groups or subfamilies: the yellow perch, the walleyes or pikeperches, and the darters. The darters are the least known, the smallest and by far the most numerous, since nearly 100 species of these small fishes occur in the lakes and streams of temperate North America. These elongate and largely predaceous fishes are spiny-rayed; have two distinct dorsal fins, the first one spiny; one or two spines precede the anal rays; pelvic fins thoracic; scales ctenoid; lateral line usually present.

YELLOW WALLEYE
Stizostedion vitreum vitreum (Mitchill)

Other common names: Pickerel, yellow pickerel, yellow pikeperch, walleye, walleye pike, dore, doré jaune.

Distinguishing features: The body of the yellow walleye is elongate and robust. On the jaws are many strong sharp teeth—the canine teeth especially are strong and conspicuous. The eye is large and somewhat opaque. The cheek is smooth and scaleless or almost so. The body is olive-brown or dark brown in colour. There are numerous flecks or spots of gold or yellow coloration sprinkled over the body and on the head. The first or spiny dorsal fin, which is dark or smoky in colour, has a distinct black blotch on the membrane between the last 2 or 3 spines. The pelvic fins are creamy-white in colour. The lower lobe of the caudal fin has a distinct creamy-white margin.

Size: The average weight of the yellow walleye is approximately 3 pounds but specimens in excess of 5 pounds are not uncommon. The largest size on record for Ontario is a 23-pound, 9-ounce fish. It was caught in the Moon River, Parry Sound District, in 1950 by Ontario Department of Lands and Forests personnel.

Occurrence: The yellow walleye occurs northward in Quebec to the Hudson Bay drainage system, and throughout Ontario northward to Hudson Bay. Westward its range extends to British Columbia and the Northwest Territories.

Life history and habits: The yellow walleye inhabits lakes and large rivers. Spawning takes place in the spring, shortly after the break-up of the ice. The eggs, when deposited, are deserted by the spawning fish. It often ascends streams, spawning in the shallow water over a gravelly bottom. It also spawns in the shallow waters of lakes on sandy, gravelly, or stony shoals. During most of the year, the yellow walleye inhabits shallow water, but may seek deeper cool water in late summer.

Food: The food consists largely of other fishes, such as yellow perch, various species of minnows, suckers, and, in deep water, ciscoes. In summer large numbers of mayflies are eaten.

Comments: The yellow pikeperch is highly regarded by both anglers and commercial fishermen and is one of the most important commercial species in our fresh waters. The Ontario commercial catch has averaged about 4 million pounds annually since 1960, ranking about third in importance after perch and smelt. The white flesh is widely esteemed.

SAUGER
Stizostedion canadense (Smith)

Other common names: Eastern sauger, sand pike, sand pickerel, doré noir.

Distinguishing features: The body of the sauger is slender and almost cylindrical. The head and mouth are large. On the jaws are many strong sharp teeth. The canine teeth are prominent. Although the sauger resembles the yellow walleye, it may be distinguished from it by the presence of 2 or 3 rows of distinct black spots on the membranes of the first, or spiny, dorsal fin. In addition, the cheek of the sauger is covered with rough scales. The back of this species is brown or gray in colour. The sides are usually yellow, overlaid with dark brown patches or blotches. These blotches do not form a regular pattern. The pelvic and anal fins are lightly sprinkled with dark speckles but the fins tend to be milky white. There are dark brown vertical bars on the caudal fin.

Size: The average weight of the sauger is less than a pound. It seldom attains a weight of 2 pounds.

Occurrence: The sauger occurs in the St. Lawrence River basin, and throughout the Great Lakes. It is found throughout Ontario, northward to the Hudson Bay watershed. In Ontario waters, the sauger formerly reached its greatest abundance in Lake Erie and occasionally is quite abundant in shallow inland lakes.

Life history and habits: The sauger is primarily a lake fish but it also inhabits large sluggish rivers. It spawns in the spring of the year. The eggs are deposited in shallow water and are then abandoned by the parent fish. The sauger grows more slowly than the yellow walleye and does not attain as large a size as the latter species.

Food: It is a carnivorous fish, feeding on smaller fishes and especially those found close to the bottom. Large numbers of aquatic insects may also be eaten, particularly during the summer months.

Comments: The sauger is of value as a commercial species, but it has been destroyed in Lake Erie and is now taken commercially in Ontario, largely in inland waters. It is sometimes caught by anglers but it is not regarded as a popular game fish. The flesh is white, firm, and flavorous.

YELLOW PERCH
Perca flavescens (Mitchill)

Other common names: Perch, lake perch, perchaude.

Distinguishing features: The body of the perch is laterally compressed and distinctl deeper than wide. There are many fine teeth on the jaws, but long canine teeth ar absent. It may be distinguished on the basis of its colour alone. The body is yellov or green in colour. On the sides are 7 (sometimes 6 or 8) broad, dark vertical bar which extend almost to the belly. The membrane between the spines of the first dorsa fin is usually dark or "smoky." The pectoral fins are light in colour, the pelvic fins pal or bright orange.

Size: The yellow perch is of medium to small size. Its average weight varies wit the environment but is usually 4 to 10 ounces. Individuals caught in the Great Lake may exceed a pound in weight and in Saskatchewan weights to 3 pounds have bee reported.

Occurrence: The yellow perch is found in many parts of North America. In easter Canada it occurs in Nova Scotia, New Brunswick, and Quebec, and in Ontario north ward to the Hudson Bay watershed. In Quebec it occurs eastward to Bay Comeat It is especially common in the Great Lakes drainage.

Life history and habits: The yellow perch spawns in shallow water in the spring c the year, usually in April or May. The eggs are expelled in rope-like strands and ar embedded in a gelatinous sheath or covering. They hatch in approximately three week (at a temperature of 45°F). No parental care is given by the adults. The adult usually move about in schools. In the spring of the year schools of yellow perch ma leave the lakes and ascend tributary streams. Although it is often found in smal bodies of water, the yellow perch is essentially a lake fish.

Food: The principal food items of the yellow perch are animal plankton, aquati insects, and fishes.

Comments: It is eaten in large numbers by many of our most important game fishe Because of this role of providing food for larger fish, the yellow perch is of inestimabl value in the economy of our waters. It is also of considerable commercial importanc in the Great Lakes, where in 1964 over 9 million pounds, worth 1¾ million dollars were landed in Ontario. The flesh has a delicious flavour and is highly esteemed. Som workers refer the perch to the species *P. fluviatilis* Linnaeus.

BLACKSIDE DARTER
Percina maculata (Girard)

Distinguishing features: The body of the blackside darter is thickset and elongate. he mouth is large and extends to beneath the front of the eye. Along the midline of ᴀe sides are a series of black, oblong blotches which are joined together. These lateral ᴌotches are continuous with a black band that extends across the gill cover and ᴋound the snout. At the base of the caudal fin is a round black spot. The lateral line complete.

Size: The average length of the blackside darter is 2¼ inches. It seldom attains inches in length.

Occurrence: The blackside darter occurs only in the southwestern part of Ontario, ᴀ Lake Erie, Lake St. Clair, southern Lake Huron, and their tributary streams.

Life history and habits: It lives in sluggish, often muddy, waters, usually on silted ᴋ muddy bottoms of streams. Spawning occurs in the spring of the year.

Food: The food of the blackside darter consists mainly of aquatic insects.

THE DARTERS

The darters, which occur only in North America, are small members of the perch ᴀmily (which includes the yellow perch, walleyes, and sauger). Although approxi-ᴌately 100 species have been described, only 11 of these occur in eastern Canada, the ᴈmaining species being confined to the United States and Mexico. Like the other ᴀembers of the perch family, they have 2 dorsal fins, one spiny and one soft-rayed. 'he darters are distinguished from the other members of the perch family by their ᴌall size and rounded caudal fins. They swim by darting swiftly from one place to ᴀother, as their name suggests. They are never seen suspended in the water but spend ᴌost of their time on the bottom. In Quebec these fishes are called les dards.

RIVER DARTER
Percina shumardi (Girard)

Distinguishing features: The river darter is a robust-bodied fish with 9 or 10 distinct brown vertical bars or blotches along the sides. On the olive-brown back are 7 or 8 indistinct saddle marks. The cheeks and opercles are usually without scales and the lateral line is complete. There are two characteristic distinguishing features on the first dorsal fin—a small black spot on the front of the fin behind the first spine, and a larger and more conspicuous blotch which extends across the last 3 spines of the fin. Beneath the eye is a broad black vertical bar.

Size: It attains a length of 2¼ inches but the average length is about 2 inches.

Occurrence: The river darter is not common in Ontario waters. It occurs, sparingly, in the western Lake Erie region and in the Rainy River and Kenora districts of western and northern Ontario.

Life history and habits: The river darter lives only in lakes and large rivers. It spawns in the spring of the year.

Food: The food consists mainly of aquatic insects.

CHANNEL DARTER
Percina copelandi (Jordan)

Distinguishing features: The body of the channel darter resembles that of the more common Johnny darter. The body is slender, almost round in cross-section. There are brown speckles on the back. Along the midline of the side are a series of small brown oblong (sometimes round) blotches, which are frequently joined together by a thin brown line. The fins are clear or only lightly speckled.

Size: The channel darter attains a length of 1¾ inches.

Occurrence: This darter is not common in Canadian waters, being more common in the warmer waters to the south. It has been reported from the upper St. Lawrence River in the vicinity of Montreal, and in Ontario, on sand and gravel beaches near Port Burwell, Erieau, and Point Pelee in Lake Erie, and from the Detroit River.

Life history and habits: Studies of the channel darter in the United States indicate that it prefers lakes and the deep waters of large rivers. Spawning occurs in the spring of the year.

Food: Aquatic insects and plankton constitute the principal foods.

Comments: It is called petit-gris des chenaux in French.

L O G P E R C H
Percina caprodes (Rafinesque)

Other common names: Zebra fish, dard-perche.

Distinguishing features: The body of the logperch is slender and slightly deepe
than wide. The bluntly pointed snout projects over the small mouth. The body colou
is gray-green, with 14 to 16 dark vertical bars. Alternate bars are longer and darke
and are expanded (drop-like) at the lower ends. There is a round and distinct blac
spot at the base of the caudal fin.

Size: The logperch is the largest of the darters. It may attain a length of 5½ inche
but 3½ inches is the average length.

Occurrence: It occurs in the upper St. Lawrence River system (eastward at least t
Nabisipi River, Quebec), in the Lake Champlain drainage, and throughout all of Ontari
from the Great Lakes northward to Hudson Bay. Westward to Saskatchewan.

Life history and habits: The logperch frequents the sandy or gravelly shallow wate
of lakes and large rivers. It is also found in the lower reaches of small streams. Spawnin
takes place in the spring of the year, when the eggs are deposited on the bottom an
left unguarded.

Food: The food of the logperch consists of plankton (small crustaceans) and aquat
insects.

Comments: The logperch is occasionally used by anglers for live bait, for which it
well suited as the hard, firm body bears up well on a hook.

SAND DARTER
Ammocrypta pellucida (Putnam)

Distinguishing features: The body of this darter is quite slender and elongate and lmost round in cross-section. There are 10 to 12 small, rounded, dark green spots along he midline of the sides and a similar series of spots along the midline of the back. The ody is partially naked, scales being confined to the midline of the sides. The lateral ine is complete. The fins are usually clear. The body is light-coloured and translucent.

Size: The average length of the sand darter is 2¼ inches—rarely more than 2½ inches.

Occurrence: It occurs in certain areas of the lake-like expansions of the upper St. .awrence River (particularly Lac St. Pierre) in Quebec. It is not a common fish in)ntario waters and is found only in western Lake Erie, Lake St. Clair, southern Lake Iuron, and their tributary streams.

Life history and habits: The sand darter frequents the sandy bottoms of streams and akes. It spends much of its time in the sand, with only the eyes exposed. Spawning ccurs in the spring of the year.

Food: Aquatic insects constitute the main food.

Comments: It is called dard de sable in French.

JOHNNY DARTER
Etheostoma nigrum Rafinesque

Distinguishing features: The slender body of the Johnny darter is almost round in cross-section and only slightly deeper than wide. The colour of the body is pale yellow or sometimes pale green. The back is speckled with brown or dark brown and has 5 or 6 broad dark saddle-like patches. There are dark, distinctive W-, M-, or V-shaped marks along the sides. These marks are always evident except on male fish in breeding dress, in which case the body and fins of the male are dark, almost black, in colour and hence the marks are obscured.

Size: The Johnny darter attains a length of 2 to 3 inches.

Occurrence: It is found in New Brunswick, in Quebec, throughout Ontario from the Great Lakes northward to Hudson Bay, and westward to Saskatchewan. In Ontario it is more common than any of our other darters.

Life history and habits: The Johnny darter inhabits both lakes and streams and is often common in the shallow waters of lakes. Spawning takes place in the spring. The eggs are deposited on the underside of stones and are guarded by the male.

Food: The Johnny darter eats plankton (small crustaceans), aquatic insects, and minute aquatic plants.

Comments: When abundant, Johnny darters may be utilized as food by larger fishes. On one occasion we found 5 in the stomach of a lake whitefish. It is called raseux-de terre in French.

Three subspecies of Johnny darters have been described and occur in our area—one in the Maritimes westward to eastern Lake Ontario (*E. n. olmstedi*), one in the lower Great Lakes and southwestern Ontario (*E. n. eulepis*) and one whose range extends from western Quebec and Hudson Bay region, westward to Saskatchewan (*E. n. nigrum*).

GREENSIDE DARTER
Etheostoma blennioides Rafinesque

Distinguishing features: The body of the greenside darter is robust and deep—deeper than that of the Johnny darter. The mouth is slightly overhung by the broadly rounded snout. The back is creamy or pale brown in colour and speckled with brown. On the sides are 5 or 6 large olive-brown V-shaped marks. These are especially prominent on the latter half of the body, where they extend to below the midline of the sides. There are two dark lines extending downward from the eye—one vertically and one downward and forward toward the mouth. The lateral line is complete. The sides are distinctly green in colour, quite unlike any of the other darters. The lower fins are blue-green in colour.

Size: The greenside darter grows to over 4 inches in length but 2 to 3 inches is the average length.

Occurrence: It is found only in the Lake St. Clair drainage of southwestern Ontario, especially in the Thames River system.

Life history and habits: It inhabits the stony or rocky sections of streams. Spawning takes place in the spring of the year.

Food: Aquatic insects and plankton constitute the principal food.

RAINBOW DARTER
Etheostoma caeruleum Storer

Other common names: Rainbow fish, blue darter, petit-gris arc-en-ciel.

Distinguishing features: The body of the rainbow darter is more laterally compressed and deeper than that of the other darters. On the sides of adult males are 9 to 14 vertical bars of brilliant blue or green, the spaces between the bars being yellow or orange. Green, blue, and orange coloration abounds on the head, sides, breast, and fins. The males, which are most brilliant in the spring, are more highly coloured than the females. The rainbow darter is the most colourful of our native fishes.

Size: The rainbow darter averages 2 inches in length and seldom exceeds 2½ inches.

Occurrence: This fish occurs in the upper St. Lawrence drainage of Quebec, where it is rare. In Ontario it is found in the streams emptying into western Lake Ontario, Lake Erie, Lake St. Clair, southern Lake Huron, and southern Georgian Bay.

Life history and habits: The rainbow darter lives in cool streams, preferring the fast flowing waters of stony or gravelly riffles. In the spring of the year, the eggs are deposited among the pebbles on the bottom and left unattended by the parents.

Food: Its food consists primarily of plankton (crustaceans) and aquatic insects.

Comments: Although extremely colourful, the rainbow darter does not usually adapt itself to the static waters of the average aquarium because of its need for cool, flowing water and an abundant supply of oxygen.

IOWA DARTER
Etheostoma exile (Girard)

Distinguishing features: The body of the Iowa darter is slender and laterally compressed. The back is dark brown in colour, sometimes with approximately 8 dark, narrow, saddle-shaped marks (smaller and paler than those on the Johnny darter). There are 10 to 12 brown or rust-coloured vertical bars or square patches along the sides. The dark vertical bar below the eye is distinct. The dorsal and caudal fins are heavily speckled with regularly arranged brown spots—these spots are indistinct on the lower fins. Occasional specimens (especially males caught in the spring of the year) are vividly coloured. These fish have blue or green bars between the brown bars on the sides, and the underparts are yellow; also, the lower fins are red or red-brown in colour. The first dorsal fin has a longitudinal blue band along the base, above this a red band and, finally, a narrow blue band along the outer edge.

Size: The Iowa darter averages 2 inches in length and seldom exceeds 2½ inches.

Occurrence: The Iowa darter is found in southern and western Quebec from the Lake Champlain and upper St. Lawrence River drainages westward throughout the Great Lakes and Lake of the Woods, and northward in Ontario to the James Bay watershed.

Life history and habits: The Iowa darter usually inhabits the shallow waters of lakes and rivers, where the silted bottom has a small amount of aquatic vegetation. They are occasionally found in the fast-flowing waters of rocky or gravelly streams. The eggs are laid on the bottom stones, often in crevices, in the spring of the year and abandoned by the adults.

Food: The food consists of plankton and aquatic insects.

Comments: The Iowa darter seldom occurs in sufficient abundance to constitute a significant proportion of the food of larger fishes. Its French name is petit-gris de vase.

FANTAIL DARTER
Etheostoma flabellare Rafinesque

Distinguishing features: The robust body of the fantail darter is laterally compressed and deep, even to the base of the caudal fin. The head is long and also compressed and rather pointed in front. Unlike the other darters (on which the snout usually projects), the lower jaw is equal in length to the upper jaw, or projects beyond it. The lateral line is usually complete or nearly so. The body is brown in colour. On the sides, mainly evident on the upper half, are 10 to 12 short dark vertical bars. There is a prominent black blotch located behind the head and above the base of the pectoral fin. The spines on the first dorsal fin are short and, on the males, are tipped with fleshy knobs. There are conspicuous brown bars on the second dorsal fin and the caudal fin.

Size: The fantail darter averages 2½ to 2¾ inches in length.

Occurrence: This darter occurs in the upper St. Lawrence River (at least to Lac St. Pierre) and westward in Ontario to the drainages of Lake Ontario and Lake Erie. It is rare in eastern Lake Ontario.

Life history and habits: The fantail darter is most frequently found in the riffles of streams. Spawning occurs in the spring of the year. A nest is selected beneath or among the rocks and after the eggs are laid they are guarded by the male. It is said to be the wariest and fastest swimmer of all the darters.

Food: The food consists of aquatic insects, plankton, and small molluscs.

Comments: In French it is called petit-gris barré.

LEAST DARTER
Etheostoma microperca Jordan and Gilbert

Distinguishing features: The small body of the least darter is laterally compressed. The brown or brown-green back and sides are sprinkled with darker brown spots. There are 7 or 8 squarish dark brown blotches on the sides. The lateral line is absent. The second dorsal fin and caudal fin have a barred appearance due to the presence of regularly arranged brown spots. Beneath the eye is a short dark vertical bar.

Size: The least darter is the smallest fish in our fresh waters. It attains a maximum length of 1½ inches and averages only slightly more than an inch in length.

Occurrence: In Ontario waters the least darter has been found only in the drainages of western Lake Ontario, Lake Erie, and Lake St. Clair.

Life history and habits: It inhabits the quiet, weedy parts of slow-moving creeks and streams, and spawns in the spring of the year.

Food: The food of the least darter consists of small crustaceans (plankton) and aquatic insects.

Comments: Because of its small size and limited occurrence in our waters, it is seldom caught, even by collectors.

BROOK SILVERSIDES
Labidesthes sicculus (Cope)

Other common names: Silverside, skipjack, poisson d'argent de ruisseau.

Distinguishing features: The brook silversides has a slender body and a long head which is flattened above. The snout is drawn-out and the jaws beak-like. There are 2 dorsal fins; the first, consisting of only 4 spines, is small and inconspicuous. The anal fin has a long base, almost twice the length of the second dorsal fin, both fins being relatively high in front and tapering rapidly posteriorly. The body, which is somewhat transparent, is of a pale green colour. There is a pronounced silvery lateral band along the sides.

Size: It is a small fish, averaging 2 to 3 inches in length. Occasional specimens may attain a length of 3½ inches.

Occurrence: The brook silversides occurs in the drainages of the upper St. Lawrence River and the Ottawa River, in Lake Ontario, Lake Erie, Lake St. Clair, and Georgian Bay. In certain parts of eastern Lake Ontario and in some inland lakes in Leeds County in eastern Ontario it may be very abundant, especially in late summer.

Life history and habits: It swims near the surface in lakes, bays, and expanded portions of streams and frequently assembles in large schools. Spawning takes place in the spring among aquatic vegetation.

Food: The brook silversides feeds on aquatic and terrestrial insects and plankton.

Comments: When abundant, this species is eaten in quantity by game fishes, at which time it is an important forage fish. It is occasionally used as bait by sport fishermen.

THE SILVERSIDES   family ATHERINIDAE

The silversides are slender, silvery fishes of inshore waters in temperate seas, and often occur in large schools. One of the few freshwater species ranges widely in eastern North America, including southeastern Canada. A close relative, the Atlantic silversides, *Menidia menidia*, lives in the brackish and salt waters of the southern Gulf of St. Lawrence, south to Cape Cod. Some characteristic structural features are: the two, widely separated, dorsal fins; many-rayed anal fin; pectorals high on sides; pelvics abdominal; lateral line absent.

FRESHWATER DRUM
Aplodinotus grunniens Rafinesque

Other common names: Sheepshead, freshwater sheepshead, drum, malachigan.

Distinguishing features: The body of the freshwater drum is laterally compressed. The upper outline of the body is highly arched to the dorsal fin. The lower outline is almost straight. The mouth is overhung by the snout, which distinguishes this species from the other spiny-rayed fishes. The dorsal fin is long, extending almost to the caudal fin, and is composed of a spiny-rayed part and a soft-rayed part which are separated by a distinct notch. The anal fin has two spines preceding the soft rays, the second spine being large and thick. The caudal fin is rounded and the pelvic fins terminate with hair-like filaments. The back is dark green in colour, the sides silvery, and the belly usually white. The pelvic fins are white to cream in colour, the pectoral fins clear, and the remaining fins dusky.

Size: The freshwater drum averages 1 to 2 pounds in weight but occasionally specimens weighing 10 pounds or more are taken in the Great Lakes. It has been reported to attain up to 14 pounds in Lake Abitibi and to 17 pounds in Lake Nipissing. One weighing 24 pounds was reported caught in Hay Bay, Lake Ontario, in 1964 and may be an Ontario record.

Occurrence: The freshwater drum occurs in Lake Champlain, the upper St. Lawrence River, the Ottawa River, northward to Lake Abitibi, and in the Great Lakes (except Lake Superior) westward into Manitoba. It is common in the Bay of Quinte in Lake Ontario and in Lake Erie.

Life history and habits: The freshwater drum is a bottom-living fish, preferring the mud or sand-bottomed shallow waters of lakes or large rivers. In Lake Erie, main spawning occurs after July 1 and recently spawned females have been taken as late as September. The freshwater drum is capable of producing a strange grunting sound.

Food: Its main food consists of snails and other molluscs and crayfish, which it crushes with powerful mill-like teeth (pharyngeal teeth), located in the throat.

Comments: Although not often captured by anglers, the freshwater drum is commonly taken in the catches of commercial fishermen, especially in the shallows of western Lake Erie. The flesh, although not highly esteemed, is white, flaky, and of good flavour. The large otoliths, or ear-stones, are known to many fishermen as "lucky stones." The freshwater drum is sometimes mistaken by anglers for white bass and even smallmouth bass!

THE DRUMS   family SCIAENIDAE

The drums are large, deep-bodied, compressed fishes, most abundant in shallow waters of warm seas. Some species live in fresh water and one of these is widely distributed in central and Eastern North America. The common name has arisen because of the ability to make a drumming or croaking noise, utilizing the air bladder. Hence, they are also called croakers. Some characteristic structural features are: dorsal fin divided, of two distinct fins or deeply notched, the first spiny, the second soft-rayed and longer; one or two spines in anal fin; pelvic fins thoracic; caudal seldom forked; scales ctenoid; lateral line distinct and extending onto caudal fin; lower pharyngeal (or "throat") teeth often enlarged and fused; otoliths large.

THE SCULPINS   family COTTIDAE

The freshwater sculpins are a group of small, rather grotesquely shaped fishes, represented in our waters by four species. The family (Cottidae) to which they belong is primarily marine, containing many species which occur in the cool seas of the northern hemisphere. Our species, which are bottom-living fishes, are not well known to fishermen who, except for trout fishermen, rarely have an opportunity to see them. At least two of the species are important prey of game fish. Typical scales are absent or represented by scattered tubercles or prickles which are rough to the touch.

MOTTLED SCULPIN
Cottus bairdi Girard

Other common names: Northern muddler, muddler, chabot marbré.

Description: For a general description see the slimy sculpin, *Cottus cognatus*, since these two fishes are very alike in appearance. In contrast to the slimy sculpin, this species is less slimy, and usually possesses palatine teeth. (Pelvic fin ray count, I, 4.)

Size: The average length of this fish is 2 to 3 inches.

Occurrence: It occurs in New Brunswick, Labrador, and the upper St. Lawrence River drainage, and in Ontario from the Great Lakes northward to the James Bay watershed.

Food: The principal food items are aquatic insects, crustaceans, small fishes, and aquatic vegetation.

Comments: Similar to the slimy sculpin, it forms an important part in the diet of the brook trout.

S L I M Y   S C U L P I N
Cottus cognatus Richardson

Other common names: Miller's thumb, slimy muddler, cockatouch, freshwater sculpin, chabot visqueux.

Distinguishing features: The front part of the body of the slimy sculpin is stout, tapering rapidly toward the tail. The head, eyes, and mouth are large. Palatine teeth are usually absent. There is a short spine on the gill cover. The skin is slippery, or slimy, and without scales, excepting for a patch of small prickles behind the pectoral fin. The lateral line is incomplete and terminates below the second dorsal fin. There are two dorsal fins, the first short and the second long, extending almost to the caudal fin. The anal fin is almost as large as the second dorsal fin and the pectoral fins are enlarged and wing-like. The pelvic fins are small, the body is brown (at times almost black), mottled with darker brown or black. Occasionally, there are dark, saddle-shaped bars on the back. The under surface is white. The fins (excepting the pelvic fins) are frequently barred with brown or gray. (Pelvic fin ray count usually I, 3.)

Size: The average size of the slimy sculpin is 2 to 3 inches in length but occasionally it attains a length of 4 inches.

Occurrence: The slimy sculpin occurs from Labrador, Quebec, New Brunswick, and Nova Scotia northwestward to Alaska, and from the Great Lakes northward to Hudson Bay.

Life history and habits: It is found in lakes and cool, rocky streams, frequently in association with brook trout. It is said to spawn in the spring of the year, the eggs being attached to the underside of stones and guarded by the male until they hatch.

Food: The principal food items are aquatic insects, crustaceans, small fishes and aquatic vegetation.

Comments: The slimy sculpin (and the mottled sculpin) are important food of brook trout. They are occasionally used as live bait, especially for the brook trout.

SPOONHEAD SCULPIN
Cottus ricei (Nelson)

Distinguishing features: The body is slender, particularly toward the caudal fin. The head is greatly flattened. Preoperculor spine on gill cover long, strongly curved and embedded in skin. The lateral line is complete and extends to the caudal fin. The skin is often covered with fine prickles which are rough to the touch.

Size: A length of 3 or 4 inches may be attained but lengths of 2 or 3 inches are more common.

Occurrence: This sculpin occurs in western Quebec and in Ontario throughout the Great Lakes, Lake Nipigon, Lake Abitibi, northward to Fort Severn on Hudson Bay.

Life history and habits: Spawning probably occurs in the spring. It is primarily a fish of lakes or large rivers where it often frequents the deep water.

Food: The food consists principally of plankton and aquatic insects.

Comments: The spoonhead sculpin constitutes part of the diet of the lake trout and burbot. In Quebec it is called chabot à tête plate.

DEEPWATER SCULPIN
Myoxocephalus quadricornis thompsoni (Girard)

Other common names: Scorpion fish, sculpin.

Distinguishing features: The slender body and head are somewhat elongate. Except for the pelvics, the fins are long and well developed, particularly the pectorals. The 2 dorsal fins are widely separated. The skin is smooth but the lateral line is conspicuous, raised, and chain-like in appearance, and extends almost to the caudal fin. There are 4 spines on the gill cover.

Size: This is the largest of the fresh water sculpins, attaining a maximum length of about 7 inches (specimen from Lake Ontario).

Occurrence: The deepwater sculpin occurs in the deep waters (over 100 feet) of all of the Great Lakes and in Lake Nipigon. In Lake Ontario it was common in deep water and has been caught in gill nets at depths of over 400 feet but it appears to have become rare in recent years. It has recently been reported from Cedar Lake, Algonquin Park.

Life history and habits: Spawning occurs in the spring, probably over a rocky or gravelly bottom.

Food: Plankton and aquatic insects are the principal foods.

Comments: This sculpin forms part of the diets of lake trout and burbot. It is sometimes seen by commercial fishermen in whose nets it may become entangled, but in some lakes its presence is known only because it has been found in the stomachs of lake trout and burbot. A glacial relict, this sculpin will possibly be found in other inland Canadian lakes.

THE FLATFISHES

The flatfishes (order Pleuronectiformes) are essentially marine fishes living in shallow, coastal waters throughout the world. Three species, in two families, enter the lower reaches of coastal streams in eastern Canada. The flatfishes are so named because they have become adapted to lying on one side of the bottom. The down side is called the blind side, for the eye migrates from it to the upper side, which is also pigmented. Flounders are said to be dextral (right side uppermost), or sinistral (left side uppermost).

The windowpane, *Scophthalmus aquosus* (Mitchill) (family Bothidae), is a sinistral flounder with a very thin body (hence the common name), nearly circular in shape. It is light in colour with dark spots. The dorsal fin rays, just above the eyes, are long, free of membrane and appear like fringe. The windowpane has been reported a few times from brackish estuaries or lower reaches of streams in the odd location along the Atlantic coast from Newfoundland and the Maritime Provinces.

The winter flounder, *Pseudopleuronectes americanus* (Walbaum) (family Pleuronectidae) is a dextral flounder, well known as a commercial species in Atlantic coastal waters. Inshore specimens are seldom longer than 18 inches. It can be distinguished from the smooth flounder, which is also dextral, by the scaling between the eyes, making this area rough to the touch; whereas the area between the eyes is not scaled and is smooth to the touch on the smooth flounder. The colour of the winter flounder is usually dark brown with darker spots or blotches.

The smooth flounder, *Liopsetta putnami* (Gill) (family Pleuronectidae) occurs more frequently in brackish and freshwater areas than the previously mentioned species. It has been reported occasionally from lower reaches of streams flowing into the Bay of Fundy. It is the smallest of our flounders, not exceeding 12 inches in length. Its uniformly dark colour and smooth texture will assist in distinguishing it from other flatfishes.

KEY TO FAMILIES

THE USE OF KEYS: Keys are used to assist in making an identification. These keys consist
of a series of choices in the form of couplets, numbered on the left-hand margin. To use
the key, compare the characters of the specimen in hand with the first statement. If the
statement agrees, follow the indication given at the end of the statement, which will be
either a name or the number of the next couplet. If the statement is not in agreement,
proceed to the second part of the couplet. Continue in this way until an identity is made.

1 Mouth without true jaws, instead a circular, suctorial disc; no paired fins;
7 pairs of gill openings   Lampreys, family Petromyzontidae (p. 2)

 Mouth with true jaws (i.e. upper and lower jaws present); with paired fins;
opercles (or gill covers) overlying gills   2

2 Upper and lower lobe of caudal (tail) fin, when present, of about equal size;
body covering of overlapping scales or naked; snout not paddle-like, no
barbels before mouth; skeleton bony   4

 Upper lobe of caudal (tail) fin distinctly larger than lower lobe; mouth
inferior, snout greatly extended; skeleton chiefly cartilaginous   3

3 Snout flat and greatly expanded in front, paddle-like; skin smooth
          Paddlefishes, family Polyodontidae (p. 8)

 Snout well developed but not paddle-like; 5 rows of bony plates arranged
longitudinally along body; 4 pairs of barbels before mouth
          Sturgeons, family Acipenseridae (p. 7)

4 Body strongly compressed laterally (plate-like); both eyes on one side, eyed-
side uppermost and pigmented, blind side unpigmented
     Flatfishes, families Pleuronectidae and Bothidae (p. 120)

 Body more or less of conventional shape but not excessively flattened; one
eye on each side of head   5

5 Under surface of head, between lower jaws, with strong bony plate ("gular"
plate)   Bowfins, family Amiidae (p. 11)

 Under surface of head, between the lower jaws, soft and not protected by
large bony plate   6

6 Pelvic fins present   8

 Pelvic fins absent   7

7 Body cylindrical, long and snake-like; dorsal, caudal and anal fins continuous;
no distinct caudal fin   Eels, family Anguillidae (p. 76)

 Body thin and pencil-like; dorsal fin long but not continuous with caudal fin;
distinct caudal fin   Sand lance, family Ammodytidae*

8 Adipose fin present   9

 Adipose fin absent   14

9 Body scaleless; strong pectoral and dorsal spines; long barbels about mouth
          Catfishes, family Ictaluridae (p. 71)

 Body scaled; no strong spines in fins; no long barbels about mouth 10

10 Pectoral fin tip overlaps anterior pelvic base; scales (weakly) ctenoid
          Trout-perch, family Percopsidae (p. 85)

 Pelvic fins abdominal; pectoral fin tip never reaches anterior base of pelvic fin;
scales cycloid   11

11 Pelvic axillary process absent   Smelts, family Osmeridae (p. 32)

 Pelvic axillary process present   12

*Reported only once, from Newfoundland, by Scott and Crossman (1964).

12 Mouth usually large and extending to middle of eye or beyond; teeth strong
Salmons and trouts, family **Salmonidae** (p. 15)

Mouth usually small and not extending beyond middle of eye; teeth weak
or absent   1£

13 Dorsal fin base shorter than head; dorsal rays 16 or fewer
Whitefishes, family **Salmonidae** (p. 26)

Dorsal fin base longer than head; dorsal rays 17 or more
Grayling, family **Salmonidae** (p. 32)

14 Pelvic fins abdominal (posterior to pectoral fin base)   1£

Pelvic fins thoracic or jugular (below or anterior to pectoral fin base)   2£

15 A single soft dorsal fin present, not preceded by spines   1£

Soft dorsal fin preceded by 3–10 isolated spines or by a separate spiny dorsal
of 4 slender, inconspicuous spines   2£

16 Body covered with thick, hard, glossy rhomboid scales
Gars, family **Lepisosteidae** (p. 9)

Body normally scaled or with scattered prickles or narrow plates   1£

17 Gill membranes not attached to isthmus (gill openings wide)   1£

Gill membranes broadly joined to isthmus (gill openings narrow)   2£

18 Head with some scales; body elongate; spotted, barred or dark coloured   1£

Head without scales; body laterally compressed; silvery   2£

19 Upper jaw protractile   Killifishes, family **Cyprinodontidae** (p. 78)

Upper jaw not protractile   2£

20 Jaws well developed; teeth strong; caudal fin forked
Pikes, family **Esocidae** (p. 37)

Jaws short; teeth small; caudal fin rounded
Mudminnows, family **Umbridae** (p. 36)

21 Lips thick; mouth distinctly inferior; pharyngeal teeth numerous and in one
row, comb-like; air bladder of 2 or 3 chambers
Suckers, family **Catostomidae** (p. 42)

Lips thin; mouth seldom strongly inferior (except in *Rhinichthys*); pharyngeal
teeth in 2 or 3 rows and fewer than 9 per side; air bladder of two chambers
Minnows, family **Cyprinidae** (p. 50)

22 Lateral line absent; teeth absent   Herrings, family **Clupeidae** (p. 12)

Lateral line present; teeth present   Mooneyes, family **Hiodontidae** (p. 34)

23 Body plated, naked or with prickles; pectoral fins large and conspicuous
Sculpins, family **Cottidae** (p. 116)

Body scaled (scales small and somewhat embedded in Gadidae); pectoral
fins of moderate size, not conspicuous   2£

24 Strong pelvic spines present; caudal fin rounded or only slightly forked
Sticklebacks, family **Gasterosteidae** (p. 81)

Pelvic fins without spines; caudal fin forked
Silversides, family **Atherinidae** (p. 114)

25 Chin with small but distinct median barbel   Cods, family **Gadidae** (p. 79)

Chin without small median barbel   26

26 Anal spines one or 2   27

Anal spines 3 or more   28

27 Second anal spine strong and stout and conspicuously larger than first; lateral
line extending onto caudal fin   Drums, family **Sciaenidae** (p. 115)

Second anal spine slender and not conspicuously larger than first; lateral line
not extending onto caudal fin   Perches, family **Percidae** (p. 99)

28 Opercle with a spine; 3 anal spines only; pseudobranch well developed and
obvious   Basses, family **Serranidae** (p. 86)

Opercle without a spine; 3 or more anal spines; pseudobranch concealed or
absent   Sunfishes, family **Centrarchidae** (p. 89)

KEY TO SALMONS, TROUTS, CHARS, WHITEFISHES—
FAMILY SALMONIDAE

1 Scales small, those in lateral line 115–200; teeth well developed on jaws and vomer; caudal usually truncate, occasionally forked; young (6 inches or less) with dark vertical blotches (parr marks) on sides (except *O. gorbuscha*)
SALMONS, TROUTS, CHARS (Salmoninae)   2

Scales large, those in lateral line 100 or less; teeth weakly developed or absent; caudal fin distinctly forked; parr marks absent (except *Prosopium*); colour silvery.   WHITEFISHES (Coregoninae)   8

2 Anal rays 13–19 (usually 14–16); body and caudal fin of adults with black spots   PACIFIC SALMONS, *Oncorhynchus* spp. (p. 16)

Anal rays 7–12 (usually 9–11); body and caudal fin with or without black spots   3

3 Black spots present on head and body (young *S. salar* have red spots between parr marks); scales conspicuous, fewer than 165 in lateral line; pelvic and anal fins without white leading edges; vomer flat with teeth extended backward in 2 rows   4

Light spots, not black spots, on body, these spots being pink, red, or cream in colour; lower fins with snow-white leading edges; vomer boat-shaped, teeth on the anterior part only   6

4 Caudal fin distinctly marked with radiating rows of black spots; body never with red spots; anal fin usually with 10 or 11 rays; adipose fin often with a black margin   RAINBOW TROUT, *Salmo gairdneri* (p. 19)

Caudal fin usually unspotted, never with regular rows of black spots; reddish spots sometimes on body; anal fin with 8–11 rays; adipose fin without black margin   5

5 Maxillary to below centre of eye in 6-inch fish, seldom far behind eye (except in large males); gill cover with 2 or 3 large spots only; branchiostegals usually 12; dorsal fin rays usually 11; vomerine teeth usually not well developed; small fish have red spots between parr marks; no red on adipose fin   ATLANTIC SALMON, *Salmo salar* (p. 15)

Maxillary to below last half of eye on 5-inch fish, and extending well beyond eye in larger fish; gill cover usually with many spots; branchiostegals usually 10; dorsal fin rays usually 9; vomerine teeth well developed; rust-red spots sometimes on adults and often on margin of adipose fin
BROWN TROUT, *Salmo trutta* (p. 18)

6 Caudal fin square or nearly so; dorsal and caudal fins with distinct, dark wavy lines or blotches; back usually with wavy lines (vermiculations); sides with pink or red spots, many of which have blue borders; young with 8–10 regularly arranged parr marks on sides
BROOK TROUT, *Salvelinus fontinalis* (p. 21)

Caudal fin shallow or deeply forked; dorsal and caudal fins and back plain or with light spotting; spots on sides light, sometimes pink, never with blue borders; parr marks vague or quite irregular, not well defined   7

7 Caudal fin deeply forked; dorsal and caudal fins, body and head covered with small, often bean-shaped light spots, body never brightly coloured with orange or red; parr marks quite irregular, and narrow
LAKE TROUT, *Salvelinus namaycush* (p. 23)

Caudal fin slightly or distinctly forked; dorsal and caudal fins plain, usually dusky, never with spots or wavy lines; cream or pink spots on sides only; lower half of body sometimes brightly coloured with red, orange or yellow; parr marks vague, irregular and broad
ARCTIC CHAR, *Salvelinus alpinus* (p. 20)

---

*When in the sea or in large lakes, body pigmentation is usually masked by heavy silvery coloration. The characters enumerated in the Key will be evident if the specimen is examined carefully.

8   Gill rakers short, stout, 14–19; a single, small flap of skin between nostrils
         ROUND WHITEFISHES, *Prosopium* spp.
    Gill rakers long, slender, more than 22; two small flaps of skin between
    nostrils   1

9   Lateral line scales usually 83–96; scales around caudal peduncle 22–24;
    pyloric caeca 50–116; a fish of medium size, to about 20 inches
         ROUND WHITEFISH, *Prosopium cylindraceum* (p. 28)
    Lateral line scales usually 56–66; scales around caudal peduncle 18–20;
    pyloric caeca 15–23; a small species, less than 8 inches long
         PYGMY WHITEFISH, *Prosopium coulteri* (p. 28)

10   Gill rakers usually less than 32; mouth usually inferior, being overhung by
    rounded snout (except Atlantic whitefish); body mucus ("slime") con-
    spicuous   1
    Gill rakers usually more than 32 (more commonly 40 or more); mouth
    terminal or nearly so; upper and lower jaws more or less equal; body mucus
    not conspicuous   CISCOES, or FRESHWATER HERRINGS, subgenus
    Leucichthys (9 species) (*Coregonus artedii* most widespread, p. 29)

11   Scales in lateral line less than 90 (70–85); mouth inferior, obviously over-
    hung by snout; small teeth on premaxillaries, palatines and vomer of juveniles
    (under 100 mm long) only
         LAKE WHITEFISH, *Coregonus clupeaformis* (p. 27)
    Scales in lateral line more than 90 (91–100); mouth terminal or nearly so;
    teeth on premaxillaries, palatines and vomer small but present, even on
    adults   ATLANTIC WHITEFISH, *Coregonus canadensis* (p. 26)

KEY TO MINNOWS—FAMILY CYPRINIDAE

1   Dorsal fin base long, more than 11 soft rays; dorsal and anal fins each with
    strong spine, serrated on trailing edge
    Dorsal fin base short, fewer than 11 rays; no spines in fins

2   Two pairs of long barbels on upper jaw; pharyngeal teeth molar-like
    (1,1,3–3,1,1); scales in lateral line usually more than 32; gill rakers 21–27.
    (Mirror and leather carp only partially scaled)
         CARP, *Cyprinus carpio* (p. 52)
    Barbels absent; pharyngeal teeth not molar-like (4–4); scales in lateral line
    usually less than 32; gill rakers 37–43
         GOLDFISH, *Carassius auratus* (p. 51)

3   Premaxillaries not protractile (i.e., no groove crossing midline of snout)
    Premaxillaries protractile (i.e., with groove across snout)

4   Scales in lateral line fewer than 55; lower jaw tri-lobed, its centre lobe
    tongue-shaped; body silvery, dark lateral band
         CUTLIPS MINNOW, *Exoglossum maxillingua* (p. 70)
    Scales in lateral line more than 55; lower jaw of normal shape; body flecked
    with darkened scales; mouth more or less inferior; peritoneum profusely
    brown-speckled

5   Snout long, projecting far beyond mouth; lateral band indistinct or absent
         LONGNOSE DACE, *Rhinichthys cataractae* (p. 68)
    Snout scarcely projecting beyond mouth; lateral band prominent; rusty-red
    lateral band on spawning males
         BLACKNOSE DACE, *Rhinichthys atratulus* (p. 68)

6   Maxillary with barbel (sometimes concealed in maxillary groove or absent
    on one side)
    Maxillary without a barbel   1

7   Barbel terminal and slender, at or near end of maxillary
    Barbel in front of posterior end of upper jaw, often hidden in groove below
    maxillary   1

3   Scales in lateral line more than 55; body finely stippled with black; mouth subterminal; young usually with dark lateral band
LAKE CHUB, *Couesius plumbeus* (p. 50)
Scales in lateral line fewer than 55   9

) Snout projecting only slightly beyond mouth   10
Snout projecting considerably beyond mouth   11

) Angle enclosed by scale radii about 70–75°; snout length into standard length more than 9 times   HORNYHEAD CHUB, *Hybopsis biguttata* (p. 64)
Angle enclosed by scale radii 95–105°; snout length into standard length 8 or less   RIVER CHUB, *Hybopsis micropogon* (p. 64)

1   Body with X-shaped dark spots; scales in lateral line 38–42; lower 3 or 4 rays of caudal fin not milk white
GRAVEL CHUB, *Hybopsis x-punctata* (p. 63)
Body without definite spots; scales in lateral line 37–40; lower 3 or 4 rays of caudal fin unpigmented
SILVER CHUB, *Hybopsis storeiana* (p. 63)

2   Scales in lateral line fewer than 50; young with distinct mid-lateral black band; each scale with dense pigment anteriorly
FALLFISH, *Semotilus corporalis* (p. 54)
Scales in lateral line more than 50; scales without black pigment anteriorly   13

3   A black spot near anterior base of dorsal fin, sometimes indistinct in young; upper jaw extending to vertical through front of eye; scales 52–62; silvery, no distinct spawning colours
CREEK CHUB, *Semotilus atromaculatus* (p. 55)
No black spot on dorsal fin; upper jaw not reaching a vertical through front of eye; scales 65–75 (barbel often small or absent); sides often with scattered, darkened scales; spawning males with red flanks and belly
PEARL DACE, *Semotilus margarita* (p. 53)

4   Lateral line scales more than 60   15
Lateral line scales fewer than 55   17

5   Peritoneum pale; lateral line complete, scales less than 70; body laterally compressed, snout pointed   REDSIDE DACE, *Clinostomus elongatus* (p. 67)
Peritoneum black, lateral line incomplete, scales more than 75; body rather robust, not noticeably compressed, snout blunt   16

3   Intestine with 2 crosswise coils in addition to main loop; mouth small, terminating distinctly in advance of eye; one or two dark lines, entire or broken, between lateral band and back
REDBELLY DACE, *Chrosomus eos* (p. 56)
Intestine shorter, with single main loop; mouth larger, extending almost to below anterior margin of eye; back uniformly pigmented
FINESCALE DACE, *Chrosomus neogaeus* (p. 56)

7   Abdomen behind pelvic fins with a fleshy keel lacking scales; lateral line strongly decurved, following ventral outline of body; anal fin rays 12 or 13
GOLDEN SHINER, *Notemigonus crysoleucas* (p. 57)
Abdomen behind pelvic fins rounded over and scaled; lateral line not strongly decurved; anal fin rays usually less than 12   18

3   A dark spot (sometimes faint) at front of dorsal fin, slightly above base; back flattish; first dorsal ray separated by membrane from first well-developed ray; pre-dorsal scales small, crowded   19
No dark spot at front of dorsal fin above base (a dark pigmented area at anterior base in *Notropis umbratilis*); back scarcely flattened; first dorsal ray closely attached to first well-developed ray; pre-dorsal scales usually large   20

) Lateral line incomplete; caudal spot faint; mouth terminal but small
FATHEAD MINNOW, *Pimephales promelas* (p. 58)
Lateral line complete; a distinct caudal spot; mouth subterminal
BLUNTNOSE MINNOW, *Pimephales notatus* (p. 59)

20   Mouth very small and nearly vertical; dorsal fin rays typically 9
                    PUGNOSE MINNOW, *Opsopoeodus emiliae* (p. 63)
     Mouth larger, dorsal fin rays typically 8   2

21   Anal fin rays 9–12 (rarely 8)   2
     Anal fin rays 7 or 8 (rarely 9)   2

22   Origin of dorsal fin over, or in front of, vertical through insertion of pelvic
     fins; lateral scales twice as high as wide; lower fins of males red during
     spawning   COMMON SHINER, *Notropis cornutus** (p. 60)
     Origin of dorsal fin behind vertical through insertion of pelvic fins; scales
     round or nearly so   2

23   Body deep, depth equal to or more than length of head; dorsal fin with black
     pigmented area at anterior base; sides stippled with pigment; spawning males
     have bluish body and rosy lower fins
                    REDFIN SHINER, *Notropis umbratilis* (p. 65)
     Body slender, depth much less than length of head; no black spot at base
     of dorsal fin   2

24   Snout sharp, its length more than two-thirds distance from posterior margin
     of eye to posterior margin of gill cover; pigmentation on sides usually
     bordered below by lateral line
                    ROSYFACE SHINER, *Notropis rubellus* (p. 69)
     Snout blunt, its length less than two-thirds distance from posterior margin of
     eye to posterior margin of gill cover; pigmentation on sides terminating above
     lateral line   EMERALD SHINER, *Notropis atherinoides* (p. 61)

25   Intestine short, with single main loop, mouth usually terminal   2
     Intestine elongate, coiled on right side; mouth subterminal   3

26   Dorsal fin with black blotch on membranes between posterior rays (except
     in young); eye less than one-quarter length of head in adults; snout sharp
     or pointed   SPOTFIN SHINER, *Notropis spilopterus* (p. 66)
     Dorsal fin without black bloth or membranes between posterior rays; eye
     more than one-quarter length of head in adults; snout not sharp or pointed   2

27   A large conspicuous black spot on base of caudal fin (except in large adults)
     mouth subterminal; silvery in life
                    SPOTTAIL SHINER, *Notropis hudsonius* (p. 62)
     No large conspicuous black spot on base of caudal fin; mouth usually terminal 2

28   Lateral band usually obvious, continued forward through eye and onto
     muzzle; lateral line usually incomplete   2
     Lateral band merely dusky or absent, not continued forward through eye;
     lateral line complete   3

29   Mouth very small, almost vertical; upper jaw extending only to vertical
     through nostril; lateral line nearly or quite complete; peritoneum black
                    PUGNOSE SHINER, *Notropis anogenus* (p. 70)
     Mouth larger, upper jaw reaching beyond a vertical through nostril almost to
     below eye; lateral line incomplete; peritoneum silvery   3

30   Lateral band on chin (chin black) and on premaxillaries
                    BLACKCHIN SHINER, *Notropis heterodon* (p. 67)
     Lateral band on snout but not on chin (chin not black)   3

31   Anal rays typically 8; dorsal fin located behind pelvic insertion
                    BLACKNOSE SHINER, *Notropis heterolepis* (p. 66)
     Anal rays typically 7; dorsal fin inserted over or before pelvic insertion
                    BRIDLED SHINER, *Notropis bifrenatus* (p. 65)

N. chrysocephalus has been described as a species distinct from *N. cornutus*; chi
usually pigmented, pre-dorsal dorso-lateral scale rows 13–16 in *chrysocephalus*; chi
usually unpigmented, pre-dorsal dorso-lateral scale rows 18–24 in *cornutus*.

2 Anal rays usually 7; no black pigment about anus or base of anal fin, nor below lateral line   SAND SHINER, *Notropis stramineus* (p. 69)

Anal rays usually 8 (sometimes 9); black pigment about anus and base of anal fin; pigmentation extending below lateral line

MIMIC SHINER, *Notropis volucellus* (p. 70)

3 Dorsal fin rounded; scales with about 20 radii in adult; colour brassy

BRASSY MINNOW, *Hybognathus hankinsoni* (p. 63)

Dorsal fin somewhat falcate; scales with about 10 radii in adult; colour silvery   SILVERY MINNOW, *Hybognathus nuchalis* (p. 63)

FURTHER REFERENCES

BACKUS, R. H. 1957. Fishes of Labrador. Bull. Amer. Mus. Nat. Hist., 113(4) 273–337.

CROSSMAN, E. J., and R. G. FERGUSON. 1963. The first record from Canada of *Minytrem melanops*, the spotted sucker. Copeia 1963: 186–187.

CURTIS, BRIAN. 1948. The life story of the fish. Harcourt, Brace and Co., New Yorl 284 pp.

DOBIE, J. R., O. L. MEEHEAN, and G. N. WASHBURN. 1948. Propogation of minnow and other bait species. U.S. Dept. of Interior, Fish and Wildlife Service, Cir. 1: 113 pp. (Revised 1956).

DYMOND, J. R., 1939. The fishes of the Ottawa Region. Roy. Ont. Mus. Zool Contrib. No. 15, 43 pp.

EDDY, S., and T. SURBER. 1947. Northern fishes. Univ. Minnesota Press. 276 pp.

EVERHART, W. HARRY. 1950. Fishes of Maine. Dept. Inland Fisheries and Gam Maine. 53 pp.

FORBES, S. A., and R. E. RICHARDSON. 1920. The fishes of Illinois. Dept. Registratic and Education, Illinois. 357 pp.

HARLAN, J. R., and E. B. SPEAKER. 1951. Iowa fish and fishing. State Conservatic Commission, Iowa. 237 pp. (Revised 1956).

HUBBS, CARL L., and G. P. COOPER. 1936. Minnows of Michigan. Cranbrook Inst. Sc: Bull. No. 8, 95 pp.

HUBBS, CARL L., and KARL F. LAGLER. 1947. Guide to the fishes of the Great Lak« and tributary waters. Cranbrook Inst. Sci. 187 pp. (Revised 1958).

LA MONTE, FRANCESCA. 1945. North American game fishes. Doubleday, Doran an Co., New York. 202 pp.

LEGENDRE, VIANNEY. 1954. Key to game and commercial fishes of the province « Quebec: The freshwater fishes. Game and Fisheries Dept., Quebec, and Sociéि Canadienne d'Ecologie, Univ. Montreal. 180 pp. (Fr. and Eng. eds.).

LEIM, A. H., and W. B. SCOTT. 1966. Fishes of the Atlantic coast of Canada. Fisl Res. Bd. Canada, Bull. 155, 485 pp.

LIVINGSTONE, D. A. 1951. The fresh water fishes of Nova Scotia. Proc. Nova Scotia Inst. Sci., vol. 23, part 1, 90 pp.

MACKAY, H. H. 1963. Fishes of Ontario. Ont. Dept. Lands and Forests. 300 pp.

McCRIMMON, H. R. 1956. Fishing in Lake Simcoe. Ont. Dept. Lands and Forest 137 pp.

MELANÇON, CLAUDE. 1946. Les poissons de nos eaux. Granger Frères Ltd., Montrea 250 pp.

NASH, C. W. 1908. Checklist of the fishes of Ontario in Manual of Vertebrates « Ontario. Printed by order of the Legislative Assembly of Ontario, Warwick Brc and Rutter, Toronto. 122 pp.

NORMAN, J. R. 1932. A history of fishes. Ernest Benn Ltd., London; Bouverie Hous E.C.4. 463 pp. (Revised by P. H. Greenwood, 1963).

RADFORTH, ISOBEL. 1944. Some considerations on the distribution of fishes in Ontari Roy. Ont. Mus. Zool., Contrib. No. 25, 116 pp.

RYDER, R. A., W. B. SCOTT, and E. J. CROSSMAN. 1964. Fishes of northern Ontari north of the Albany River. Roy. Ont. Mus., Life Sci. Contrib. No. 60, 30 pp.

SCHULTZ, LEONARD P., and E. M. STERN. 1948. The ways of fishes. D. van Nostran Company, Inc., Toronto, New York, London. 264 pp.

SCOTT, W. B., and E. J. CROSSMAN. 1959. The freshwater fishes of New Brunswick: checklist with distributional notes. Roy. Ont. Mus. Zool. Palaeo., Contrib. No. 5 37 pp.

SCOTT, W. B. 1963. A review of the changes in the fish fauna of Ontario. Trans. Ro Can. Inst., 34, pt. 2: 111–125.

SCOTT, W. B., and E. J. CROSSMAN. 1964. Fishes occurring in the fresh water of Nev foundland. Dept. Fisheries, Ottawa, and Roy. Ont. Mus. Contrib. No. 58, Toront 124 pp.

INDEX

Where there are more than one page reference, bold figures indicate the main description. Page number of family account is shown in brackets.

chigan à grande bouche, 91
chigan à petite bouche, 89
cipenser brevirostrum, 8
  fulvescens, 7
  oxyrhynchus, 8
cipenseridae, [8]
lewife, 13
losa pseudoharengus, 13
  sapidissima, 12
lose à gésier, 14
lose d'Amérique, 12
lpine char, 20
mbloplites rupestris, 92
merican brook lamprey, 5
merican burbot, 80
merican eel, 77
merican shad, 12
merican smelt, 32
mia calva, 11
mie, 11
miidae, [11]
mmocrypta pellucida, 107
nguilla anguilla, 76
  rostrata, 77
nguille d'Amérique, 77
nguillidae, [76]
peltes quadracus, 83
plodinotus grunniens, 115
rctic char, 20
rctic grayling, 32
rctic salmon, 20
therinidae, [114]
tlantic eel, 77
tlantic salmon, 15
tlantic silversides, 114
tlantic sturgeon, 8
tlantic tomcod, 79
tlantic whitefish, 26
urora trout, 21

ait minnows, 50
anded killifish, 78
ar blanc, 87
ar d'Amérique, 86
arbotte brune, 72
arbotte des rapides, 74
arbue, 73
ass, 88
  black, 89
  calico, 97
  green, 91
  largemouth, 91
  largemouth black, 91

northern rock, 92
Oswego, 97
redeye, 92
rock, 92
silver, 87, 98
smallmouth, 89
smallmouth black, 89
speckled, 97
strawberry, 97
striped, 86
striper, 86
white, 87, 98
Basses, [86]
baveux, 62
beaverfish, 11
bec-de-lièvre, 70
bigmouth buffalo, 46
billfish, 9, 10
black bass, 89
  largemouth, 91
  smallmouth, 89
black bullhead, 76
black crappie, 97
black mullet, 49
black redhorse, 49
black sucker, 44
blackchin shiner, 67
blackfin, 32
blackfin cisco, 30, 32
blackhead minnow, 58
blacknose dace, 68
blacknose shiner, 66
blackside darter, 103
blackspotted stickleback, 82
bloat, 31
bloater, 31
bloodsucker, 2
"blue," 99
blue darter, 110
blue pickerel, 99
blue pike, 99
blue pikeperch, 99
blue sunfish, 93
blue walleye, 99
blueback, 29
bluegill, 93
bluegill sunfish, 93
bluntnose minnow, 59
Bothidae, 120
bottlefish, 28
bowfin, 11
Bowfins, [11]
brassy minnow, 63

bream, 57, 93
brême, 42
bridled shiner, 65
brindled madtom, 75
broad mullet, 42
brochet d'Amérique, 38
brochet maillé, 37
brochet vermiculé, 38
brook lamprey, 5, 6
    American, 5
    Michigan, 6
    northern, 6
brook silversides, 114
brook stickleback, 81
brook trout, 21
    common, 21
    eastern, 21
brook trout hybrid, 25
brown bullhead, 72
brown trout, 18
    English, 18
    European, 18
    German, 18
buffalo, bigmouth, 46
bullhead, 71, 72, 76
    black, 76
    brown, 72
    common, 72
    yellow, 71
burbot, 80
    American, 80
butterfish, 57

calico bass, 97
Carassius auratus, 51
carp, 42, 52
    European, 52
    German, 52
    golden, 51
    leather, 52
    mirror, 52
    smoked, 52
carpe, 52
Carpiodes cyprinus, 42
carpsucker, quillback, 42
catfish, 72, 73, 74
    channel, 73
    Great Lakes channel, 73
    lake, 73
Catfishes, [71]
catostome noir commun, 44
Catostomidae, [42]
Catostomus catostomus, 45
    commersoni, 44
caviar, 8, 9, 12
central mudminnow, 36
Centrarchidae, [90]
chabot à tête plate, 118
chabot marbré, 116
chabot visqueux, 117
chain pickerel, 37
channel cat, 73
channel catfish, 73

Great Lakes, 73
channel darter, 105
char, 20
    alpine, 20
    arctic, 20
    European, 20
charr, 20
Chars, whitefishes, salmons, trouts, [16]
    key to, 123
chat-fou, 75
chatte de l'est, 57
chinook salmon, 17
Chrosomus eos, 56
    neogaeus, 56
chub, 32, 54, 55
    common, 55
    creek, 55
    deepwater, 31
    gravel, 63
    hornyhead, 64
    lake, 50
    lake northern, 50
    longjaw, 31
    northern, 50
    river, 64
    shortjaw, 30
    silver, 54, 63, 85
chubs, 30
chubsucker, creek, 43
    lake, 43
chum salmon, 17
cisco, 29
    blackfin, 30, 32
    common, 29
    deepwater, 31
    longjaw, 31
    Nipigon, 30
    shallowwater, 29
    shortnose, 30
ciscoes, 26
    deep water, 30
Clinostomus elongatus, 67
Clupeidae, [12]
coast rainbow trout, 19
coaster, 21
cockatouch, 117
cod, freshwater, 80
    Tommy, 79
Cods, [80]
coho, 17
coho salmon, 17
common brook trout, 21
common bullhead, 72
common chub, 55
common cisco, 29
common eel, 77
common emerald shiner, 61
common garpike, 10
common lake trout, 23
common shiner, 60
common sucker, 44
common sunfish, 94
common white sucker, 44

common whitefish, 27
comments, viii
copper redhorse, 48
corégone de lac, 27
Coregonidae, 16
Coregonus, 26
  alpenae, 31
  artedii, 29
  canadensis, 26
  clupeaformis, 27
  coulteri, 28
  hoyi, 30, 31
  johannae, 30, 31
  kiyi, 32
  nigripinnis, 30, 32
  nipigon, 30
  reighardi, 30
  zenithicus, 30
Cottus bairdi, 116
  cognatus, 117
  ricei, 118
Cottidae, [116]
Couesius plumbeus, 50
crapet à oreilles bleues, 93
crapet calicot, 97
crapet de roche, 92
crapet-soleil, 94
crappie, 97, 98
  black, 97
  white, 98
"crazy fish," 13
creek chub, 55
creek chubsucker, 43
creek shiner, 60
Culaea inconstans, 81
cutlips, 70
Cyprinidae, [50]
  key to, 124
Cyprinodontidae, [78]
Cyprinus carpio, 52

dace, blacknose, 68
  finescale, 56
  horned, 55
  longnose, 68
  northern, 53
  pearl, 53
  redbelly, 56
  redside, 67
dard de sable, 107
dard-perche, 106
dards, 103
darter, blackside, 103
  blue, 110
  channel, 105
  fantail, 112
  greenside, 109
  Iowa, 111
  Johnny, 108
  least, 113
  rainbow, 110
  river, 104
  sand, 107

darters, 103
deep water ciscoes, 30
deepwater chub, 31
deepwater cisco, 31
deepwater sculpin, 119
distinguishing features, *vii*
dogfish, 11
  freshwater, 11
doogler, 74
dore, 100
doré jaune, 100
doré noir, 101
Dorosoma cepedianum,14
drum, 115
  freshwater, 115
Drums, [116]

ear-stones, 115
eastern brook trout, 21
eastern pickerel, 37
eastern sauger, 101
eastern speckled trout, 21
eel, 77
  American, 77
  Atlantic, 77
  common, 77
Eels, freshwater, [76]
eelpout, 80
emerald shiner, 61
  common, 61
  lake, 61
English brown trout, 18
éperlan d'Amérique, 32
épinoche à cinq épines, 81
épinoche à neuf épines, 84
épinoche à quatre épines, 83
épinoche à trois épines, 82
épinoche tachetée, 82
Erimyzon oblongus, 43
  sucetta, 43
Esocidae, [37]
Esox americanus americanus, 38
  americanus vermiculatus, 38
  lucius, 39
  masquinongy, 40
  niger, 37
  vermiculatus, 38
esturgeon à museau court, 8
esturgeon de lac, 7
esturgeon noir, 8
Etheostoma blennioides, 109
  caeruleum, 110
  exile, 111
  flabellare, 112
  microperca, 113
  nigrum, 108
  nigrum eulepis, 108
  nigrum nigrum, 108
  nigrum olmstedi, 108
European brown trout, 18
European carp, 52
European char, 20
Exoglossum maxillingua, 70

fallfish, 54
families, key to, 121
fantail darter, 112
fathead minnow, 58
fine-scaled sucker, 45
finescale dace, 56
five-spined stickleback, 81
flatfishes, 120
flounder, smooth, 120
    winter, 120
food, vii
fourspine stickleback, 83
freshwater herring, 26, 29
freshwater cod, 80
freshwater dogfish, 11
freshwater, drum, 115
Freshwater eels, [76]
freshwater killifish, 78
freshwater sculpin, 117
freshwater sheepshead, 115
freshwater smelt, 32
frost-fish, 28
frost fish, 79
Fundulus diaphanus, 78
    heteroclitus, 79

Gadidae, [80]
gar, 10
    longnose, 10
    shortnose, 9
    spotted, 9
gar pike, 10,
Gars, [10]
gaspareau, 13
gaspereau, 13
Gasterosteidae, [81]
Gasterosteus aculeatus, 82
    wheatlandi, 82
German brown trout, 18
German carp, 52
gizzard fish, 27
gizzard shad, 14
golden carp, 51
golden mullet, 49
golden redhorse, 49
golden shiner, 57
goldeye, 35
    smoked, 35
    Winnipeg, 35
goldfish, 51
goujon à fines écailles, 56
goujon à long nez, 68
goujon à nez noir, 68
goujon à ventre rouge, 56
grand brochet, 39
grass pickerel, 37, 38
grass pike, 37, 39
gravel chub, 63
gray trout, 23
grayback, 29
grayling, arctic, 32
Great Lakes channel catfish, 73
Great Lakes longear sunfish, 95

Great Lakes muskellunge, 41
Great Lakes trout, 23
Great Lakes whitefish, 27
great northern pike, 39
greater redhorse, 48
green bass, 91
green sunfish, 95
greenside darter, 109
grilse, 16
grindle, 11
gular plate, 11

hareng de lac, 29
Hearne's salmon, 20
herring, fresh water, 29
    lake, 29
    shoalwater, 29
    smoked, 30
    toothed, 34
Herrings, [12]
hickory shad, 14
Hiodon alosoides, 35
    tergisus, 34
Hiodontidae, [34]
hog sucker, 46
horned dace, 55
horned pout, 72
hornyhead chub, 64
Hybognathus hankinsoni, 63
    nuchalis, 63
Hybopsis biguttata, 64
Hybopsis storeriana, 63
    x-punctata, 63
hybrid, brook trout, 25
    lake trout, 25
    muskellunge, 41
Hypentelium nigricans, 46

ice fishing, 27, 33
Ichthyomyzon fossor, 6
    unicuspis, 4
Ictaluridae, [71]
Ictalurus melas, 76
    natalis, 71
    nebulosus, 72
    punctatus, 73
Ictiobus cyprinellus, 46
identification service, viii
inland whitefish, 27
Iowa darter, 111

jack, 39
jackfish, 39
jackpike, 39
Johnny darter, 108

Kamloops trout, 19, 20
killifish, 78
    banded, 78
    freshwater, 78
Killifishes, [78]
king salmon, 17
kiyi, 32
kokanee, 17

Labidesthes sicculus, 114
lake catfish, 73
lake chub, 50
    northern, 50
lake chubsucker, 43
lake emerald shiner, 61
lake herring, 29
lake northern chub, 50
lake perch, 102
lake shad, 14
lake shiner, 61
lake sturgeon, 7
lake trout, 23
    common, 23
lake trout decline, 24
lake trout hybrid, 25
lake whitefish, 27
lamper, 2, 4, 5
lamper eel, 2, 4, 5
Lampetra lamottei, 5
lamprey, 2
    American brook, 5
    brook, 5, 6
    marine, 2
    Michigan brook, 6
    northern, 4
    northern brook, 6
    sea, 2
    silver, 4
Lampreys, [3]
lamprey control, 3
lamproie américaine de ruisseau, 5
lamproie argentée, 4
lamproie de mer, 2
lamproie de ruisseau du nord, 6
landlocked, 2
landlocked salmon, 15
laquaiche argentée, 34
laquaiche aux yeux d'or, 35
largemouth, 91
largemouth bass, 91
largemouth black bass, 91
lawyer, 80
least darter, 113
leather carp, 52
lépisosté osseux, 10
Lepisosteidae, [10]
Lepisosteus oculatus, 9
    osseus, 10
Lepomis auritus, 96
    cyanellus, 95
    gibbosus, 94
    macrochirus, 93
    megalotis, 95
    megalotis peltastes, 95
Leucichthys, 26
    johannae, 31
life history and habits, *vii*
ling, 80
Liopsetta putnami, 120
little pickerel, 38
Loch Leven trout, 18
loche, 80

logperch, 106
longear sunfish, 95
    Great Lakes, 95
longjaw chub, 31
longjaw cisco, 31
longnose dace, 68
longnose gar, 10
longnose sucker, 45
Lota lota, 80
lotte, 80
"lucky stones", 115
lunge, 40

mackinaw trout, 23
madtom, brindled, 75
    tadpole, 75
malachigan, 115
maria, 80
marine lamprey, 2
Marston's trout, 20, 21
maskinonge, 40
maskinongé, 40
méné à grosse tête, 58
méné à longues nageoires, 70
méné à menton noir, 67
méné à nez noir, 66
méné à tête rose, 69
méné argenté, 63
méné bleu, 66
méné de lac, 50
méné de ruisseau, 60
méné de sable, 69
méné d'herbe, 65
méné émeraude, 61
méné laiton, 63
méné perlé du nord, 53
Menidia menidia, 114
menominee whitefish, 28
ménomini, 28
methy, 80
meunier, 45
Michigan brook lamprey, 6
Microgadus tomcod, 79
Micropterus dolomieui, 89
    salmoides, 91
Miller's thumb, 117
mimic shiner, 70
minnow, 78
    blackhead, 58
    bluntnose, 59
    brassy, 63
    fathead, 58
    pugnose, 63
    silvery, 63
    spottail, 62
Minnows, [50]
    key to, 124
Minytrema melanops, 43
mirror carp, 52
mooneye, 34
Mooneyes, [34]
mottled sculpin, 116
mountain trout, 23

Moxostoma anisurum, 48
  carinatum, 49
  duquesnei, 49
  erythrurum, 49
  hubbsi, 48
  macrolepidotum, 47
  spp., 47
  valenciennesi, 48
moxostome à cochon, 47
moxostome ballot, 49
moxostome blanc, 48
moxostome cuivre, 48
moxostome jaune, 48
mud cat, 72
mud fish, 36
mud pickerel, 37, 38
mud pout, 72
mud shad, 14
mud trout, 21
muddler, 116
  northern, 116
  slimy, 117
mudfish, 11
mudminnow, 36
  central, 36
Mudminnows, [36]
mulet du nord, 55
mullet, 42, 45, 47
  black, 49
  broad, 42
  golden, 49
  silver, 48
mummichog, 79
muskellunge, 40
  Great Lakes, 41
  northern, 40
muskellunge hybrid, 41
musky, 40
Myoxocephalus quadricornis thompsoni,
  119

ninespine stickleback, 84
Nipigon cisco, 30
Nocomis biguttatus, 64
  micropogon, 64
northern brook lamprey, 6
northern chub, 50
northern dace, 53
northern lamprey, 4
northern muddler, 116
northern muskellunge, 40
northern pearl dace, 53
northern pike, 39
northern redhorse, 47
northern rock bass, 92
northern sucker, 45
Notemigonus crysoleucas, 57
Notropis anogenus, 70
  atherinoides, 61
  bifrenatus, 65
  cornutus, 60
  cornutus chrysocephalus, 60
  heterodon, 67
  heterolepis, 66

  hudsonius, 62
  rubellus, 69
  spilopterus, 66
  stramineus, 69
  umbratilis, 65
  volucellus, 70
Noturus stigmosus, 75
  flavus, 74
  gyrinus, 75
  miurus, 75

occurrence, vii
omble chevalier, 20
omble de fontaine, 21
omble rouge du Québec, 21
Oncorhynchus, 17
  gorbuscha, 17
  keta, 17
  kisutch, 17
  nerka, 17
  tshawytscha, 17
onnenook, 15
Opsopoeodus emiliae, 63
Osmeridae, [33]
Osmerus mordax, 32
Oswego bass, 97
otoliths, 115
ouananiche, 15
ouitouche, 54

Pacific salmons, 17
paddlefish, 9
Paddlefishes, [8]
parr, 16
parts of fishes, names of, x
pearl dace, 53
  northern, 53
Perca flavescens, 102
perch, 88, 102
  lake, 102
  silver, 88
  white, 88
  yellow, 102
Perches, [99]
perchaude, 102
perche blanche, 88
perche-truite, 85
Percidae, [99]
Percina caprodes, 106
  copelandi, 105
  maculata, 103
  shumardi, 104
Percopsidae, [84]
Percopsis omiscomaycus, 85
petit barré, 78
petit-gris arc-en-ciel, 110
petit-gris barré, 112
petit-gris de vase, 111
petit-gris des chenaux, 105
Petromyzon marinus, 2
Petromyzontidae, [3]
pharyngeal teeth, 42, 50
pickerel, 38, 100
  blue, 99

chain, 37
    eastern, 37
    grass, 37, 38
    little, 38
    mud, 37, 38
    redfin, 38
    sand, 101
    yellow, 100
pickled minnows, 61
pigmy whitefish, 28
pike, 39
    blue, 99
    gar, 10
    grass, 37, 39
    great northern, 39
    northern, 39
    sand, 101
    walleyed, 100
Pikes, [37]
pikeperch, blue, 99
    yellow, 100
pilot fish, 28
Pimephales notatus, 59
    promelas, 58
pinfish, 83
pink salmon, 17
Pleuronectidae, 120
Pleuronectiformes, 120
pointu blanc, 28
poisson d'argent de ruisseau, 114
Polyodon spathula, 9
Polyodontidae, [8]
Pomoxis annularis, 98
    nigromaculatus, 97
poulamon, 79
pout, horned, 72
    mud, 72
preservation of fishes, viii
Prosopium cylindraceum, 28
Pseudopleuronectes americanus, 120
pugnose minnow, 63
pugnose shiner, 70
pumpkinseed, 94
Pungitius pungitius, 84
pyloric caeca, brook trout, 25
    lake trout, 25
    splake, 25
    trout-perch, 85
    whitefish, 28

Quebec red trout, 20
quillback, 42
quillback carpsucker, 42
quinnat salmon, 17

rainbow darter, 110
rainbow fish, 110
rainbow trout, 19
    coast, 19
raseux-de-terre, 108
red-sided sucker, 45
red trout, Quebec, 20, 21
redbelly dace, 56
redeye, 92

redeye bass, 92
redfin pickerel, 38
redfin shiner, 60, 65
redfin sucker, 47
redhorse, black, 49
    copper, 48
    golden, 49
    greater, 48
    northern, 47
    river, 49
    shortheaded, 47
    silver, 48
    white nose, 48
redhorse suckers, 47
redside dace, 67
Rhinichthys atratulus, 68
    cataractae, 68
river chub, 64
river darter, 104
river redhorse, 49
river whitefish, 34
roach, 57, 93
Roccus americanus, 88
    chrysops, 87
    saxatilis, 86
rock bass, 92
    northern, 92
rock sturgeon, 7
rosyface shiner, 69
round whitefish, 26, 28

Salmo gairdneri, 19
    salar, 15
    trutta, 18
salmon, 15
    arctic, 20
    Atlantic, 15
    chinook, 17
    chum, 17
    coho, 17
    Hearne's, 20
    king, 17
    landlocked, 15
    pink, 17
    quinnat, 17
    Sebago, 15
    silver, 17
    sockeye, 17
    spring, 17
"salmon trout", 23
salmons, Pacific, 17
salmons, trouts, chars, whitefishes, [16]
    key to, 123
Salmonidae, [16]
    key to, 123
Salvelinus alpinus, 20
    fontinalis, 21
    marstoni, 21
    namaycush, 23
    namaycush siscowet, 24
    timagamiensis, 22
sand darter, 107
sand pickerel, 101
sand pike, 101

sand shiner, 69
sauger, 102
    eastern, 102
saumon atlantique, 15
sawbelly, 13, 14
Schilbeodes mollis, 75
Sciaenidae, [116]
scientific name, vi
Scophthalmus aquosus, 120
scorpion fish, 119
sculpin, 119
    deepwater, 119
    freshwater, 117
    mottled, 116
    slimy, 117
    spoonhead, 118
Sculpins, [116]
sea lamprey, 2, 24
sea sturgeon, 8
sea trout, 20
Sebago salmon, 15
Semotilus atromaculatus, 55
    corporalis, 54
    margarita, 53
Serranidae, [86]
shad, 12, 13, 14
    American, 12
    gizzard, 14
    hickory, 14
    lake, 14
    mud, 14
shallowwater cisco, 29
sheepshead, 115
    freshwater, 115
shiner, 61, 97
    blackchin, 67
    blacknose, 66
    bridled, 65
    common, 60
    common emerald, 61
    creek, 60
    emerald, 61
    golden, 57
    lake, 61
    lake emerald, 61
    mimic, 70
    pugnose, 70
    redfin, 60, 65
    rosyface, 69
    sand, 69
    silver, 60
    spotfin, 66
    spottail, 62
shoalwater herring, 29
shortheaded redhorse, 47
shortjaw chub, 30
shortjaw cisco, 30
shortnose cisco, 30
shortnose gar, 9
shortnose sturgeon, 8
silver bass, 87, 98
silver chub, 54, 63, 85
silver lamprey, 4
silver mullet, 48

silver perch, 88
silver redhorse, 48
silver salmon, 17
silver shiner, 60
silver trout, 19
silverside, 114
Silversides, [114]
    Atlantic, 114
    brook, 114
silvery minnow, 63
siscowet, 24
size, vii
skipjack, 114
slimy sculpin, 117
slimy muddler, 117
smallmouth, 89
small mouth bass, 89
smallmouth black bass, 89
smelt, 32
    American, 32
    freshwater, 32
Smelts, [33]
smoked carp, 52
smoked goldeyes, 35
smoked herring, 30
smolt, 16
smooth flounder, 120
snake, 39
sockeye salmon, 17
spawneater, 62
speckled bass, 97
speckled trout, 21
    eastern, 21
splake, 25
spoonhead sculpin, 118
spotfin shiner, 66
spottail, 62
spottail minnow, 62
spottail shiner, 62
spotted gar, 9
spotted sucker, 43
spring salmon, 17
square tail, 21
steelhead, 19
steelhead trout, 19
stickleback, 83, 84
    blackspotted, 82
    brook, 81
    five-spined, 81
    fourspine, 83
    ninespine, 84
    threespine, 82
    twospine, 82
Sticklebacks, [81]
Stizosostedion canadense, 101
    vitreum glaucum, 99
    vitreum vitreum, 100
stone cat, 74
strawberry bass, 97
striped bass, 86
striper bass, 86
sturgeon, 7
    Atlantic, 8
    lake, 7

rock, 7
sea, 8
shortnose, 8
Sturgeons, [8]
sturgeon-nosed sucker, 45
sucker, 44
    black, 44
    common, 44
    common white, 44
    fine-scaled, 45
    hog, 46
    longnose, 45
    northern, 45
    redfin, 47
    red-sided, 45
    spotted, 43
    sturgeon-nosed, 45
    white, 44
Suckers, [42]
    redhorse, 47
sunfish, 93, 94
    blue, 93
    bluegill, 93
    common, 94
    Great Lakes longear, 95
    green, 95
    longear, 95
    yellow, 94
    yellowbelly, 96
Sunfishes, [90]

tadpole madtom, 75
threespine stickleback, 82
"throat teeth", 42, 50
Thymallus arcticus, 32
"tiger musky," 40
togue, 23
tomcod, 79
    Atlantic, 79
Tommy cod, 79
toothed herring, 34
topminnow, 78
touladi, 23
trout, Aurora, 21
    brook, 21
    brown, 18
    coast rainbow, 19
    common brook, 21
    common lake, 23
    eastern brook, 21
    eastern speckled, 21
    English brown, 18
    European brown, 18
    German brown, 18
    gray, 23
    Great Lakes, 23
    Kamloops, 19, 20
    lake, 23
    mackinaw, 23
    Marston's, 20, 21
    mountain, 23
    mud, 21
    Quebec red, 20
    Loch Leven, 18

rainbow, 19
    sea, 20
    silver, 19
    speckled, 21
    steelhead, 19
    Von Behr's, 18
Trouts, chars, whitefishes, salmons, [16]
    key to, 123
trout-perch, 85
Trout-perches, [84]
truite arc-en-ciel, 19
truite brune, 18
tullibee, 29
twospine stickleback, 82
tyee, 17

Umbra krameri, 36
    limi, 36
    pygmaea, 36
umbre de vase, 36
Umbridae, [36]

ventre-pourri, 59
Von Behr's trout, 18

walleye, 100
    blue, 99
    yellow, 100
walleyed pike, 100
waterbelly, 32
wendigo, 25
white bass, 87, 98
white cat, 74
white crappie, 98
white nose redhorse, 48
white perch, 88
white sucker, 44
    common, 44
whitefish, 27
    Atlantic, 26
    common, 27
    Great Lakes, 27
    inland, 27
    lake, 27
    menominee, 28
    pigmy, 28
    river, 34
    round, 28
whitefishes, 26
Whitefishes, salmons, trouts, chars, [16]
    key to, 123
windowpane, 120
Winnipeg goldeye, 35
winter flounder, 120

yellow bullhead, 71
yellow perch, 102
yellow pickerel, 100
yellow pikeperch, 100
yellow sunfish, 94
yellow walleye, 100
yellowbelly sunfish, 96

zebra fish, 106